100 Songs for Kids
Sing-Along Favorites

Arranged for Easy Piano by DAN COATES

For more information or to purchase *100 Songs for Kids* on four CDs or four cassettes, please call 1-800-621-7026

Project Manager: Carol Cuellar
Art Layout: Nancy Rehm
Album Cover Art © 2001 Madacy Kids, A Division of Madacy Entertainment Group
DAN COATES® is a registered trademark of Warner Bros. Publications

WARNER BROS. PUBLICATIONS
Warner Music Group
An AOL Time Warner Company
USA: 15800 NW 48th Avenue, Miami, FL 33014

WARNER/CHAPPELL MUSIC

CANADA: 15800 N.W. 48th AVENUE
MIAMI, FLORIDA 33014
SCANDINAVIA: P.O. BOX 533, VENDEVAGEN 85 B
S-182 15, DANDERYD, SWEDEN
AUSTRALIA: P.O. BOX 353
3 TALAVERA ROAD, NORTH RYDE N.S.W. 2113
ASIA: THE PENINSULA OFFICE TOWER, 12th FLOOR
18 MIDDLE ROAD
TSIM SHA TSUI, KOWLOON, HONG KONG

NUOVA CARISCH

ITALY: VIA CAMPANIA, 12
20098 S. GIULIANO MILANESE (MI)
ZONA INDUSTRIALE SESTO ULTERIANO
SPAIN: MAGALLANES, 25
28015 MADRID
FRANCE: CARISCH MUSICOM,
25, RUE D'HAUTEVILLE, 75010 PARIS

INTERNATIONAL MUSIC PUBLICATIONS LIMITED

ENGLAND: GRIFFIN HOUSE,
161 HAMMERSMITH ROAD, LONDON W6 8BS
GERMANY: MARSTALLSTR. 8, D-80539 MUNCHEN
DENMARK: DANMUSIK, VOGNMAGERGADE 7
DK 1120 KOBENHAVNK

Contents

AIKEN DRUM

TRADITIONAL
Arranged by DAN COATES

Aiken Drum - 2 - 1
0578B

AUNT RHODIE

TRADITIONAL
Arranged by DAN COATES

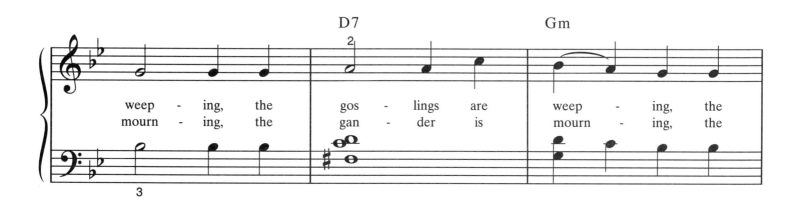

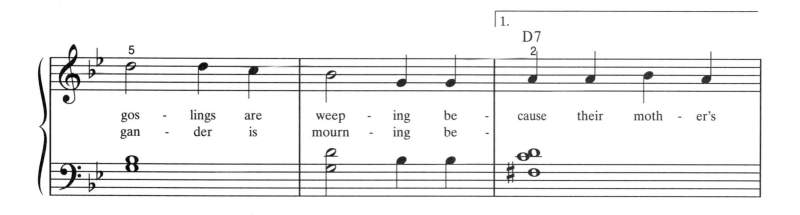

BAA-BAA BLACK SHEEP

TRADITIONAL
Arranged by DAN COATES

Moderately

THE BIG SHIPS SAIL ON THE ALI-ALI-O

TRADITIONAL
Arranged by DAN COATES

0578B

BLUETAIL FLY
(Jimmy Crack Corn)

TRADITIONAL
Arranged by DAN COATES

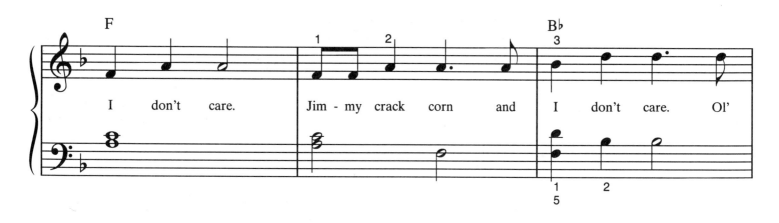

I don't care. Jim-my crack corn and I don't care. Ol'

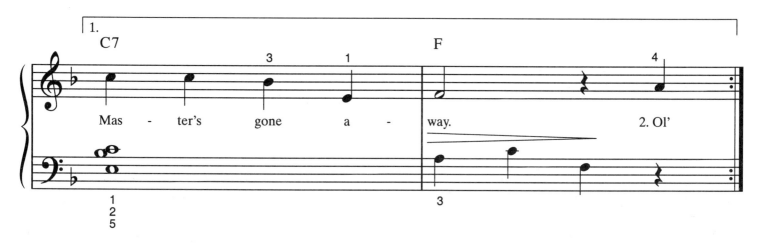

1.
Mas - ter's gone a - way. 2. Ol'

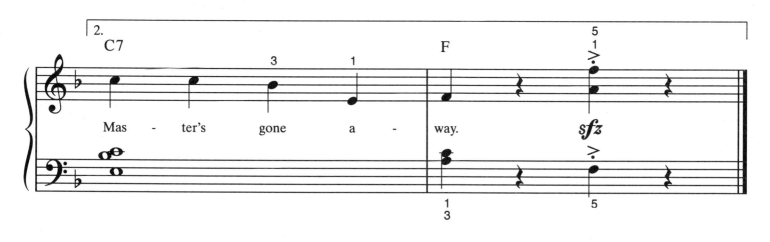

2.
Mas - ter's gone a - way. *sfz*

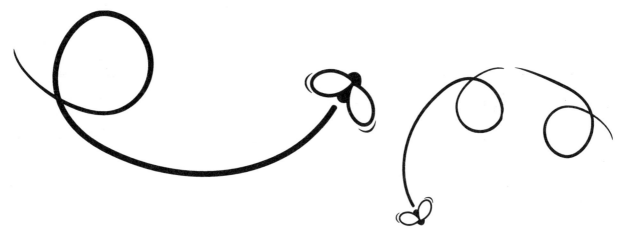

BILLY BOY

TRADITIONAL
Arranged by DAN COATES

Verse 2:
Did she ask you to come in, Billy Boy, Billy Boy?
Did she ask you to come in, charming Billy?
Yes, she asked me to come in.
There's a dimple in her chin.
She's a young thing, and cannot leave her mother.

Verse 3:
How old is she, Billy Boy, billy Boy?
How old is she, charming Billy?
Three times six and four times seven,
Twenty-eight and eleven.
She's a young thing, and cannot leave her mother.

BOBBY SHAFTO

TRADITIONAL
Arranged by DAN COATES

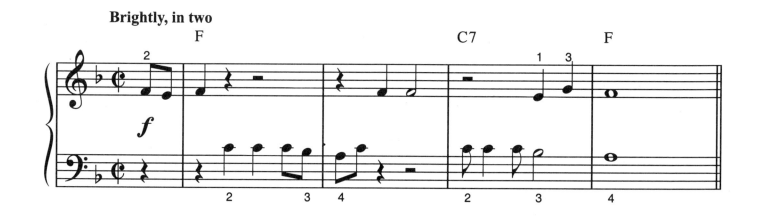

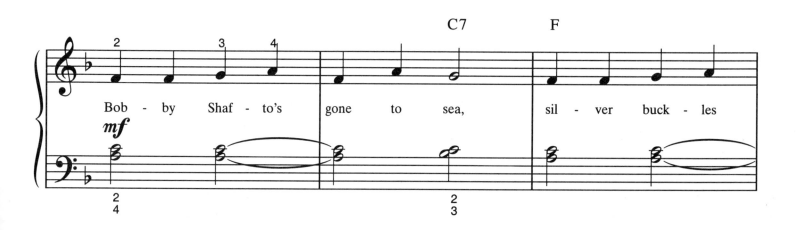

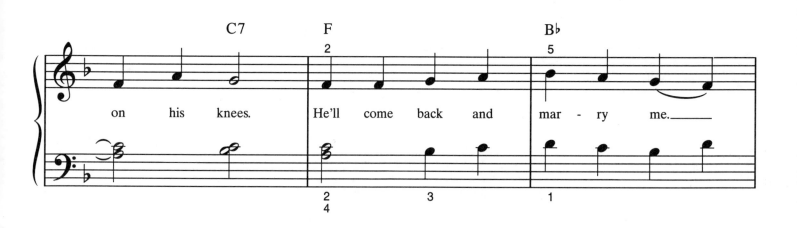

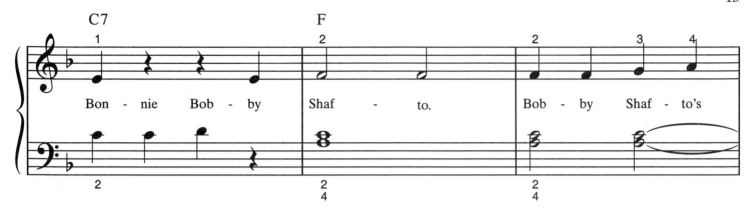

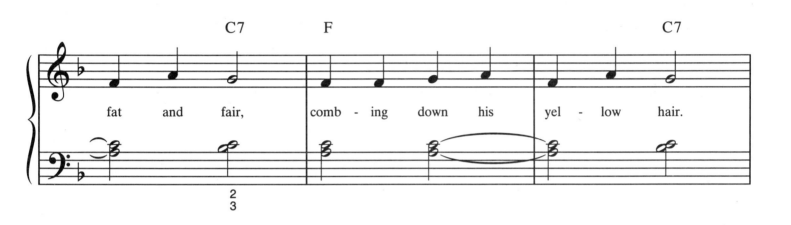

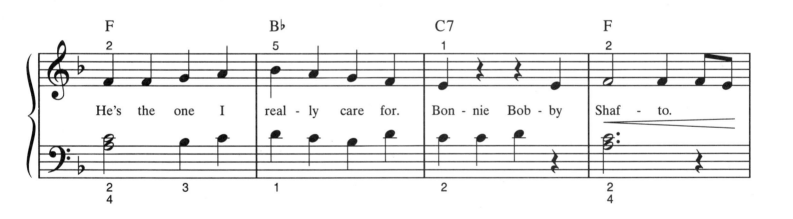

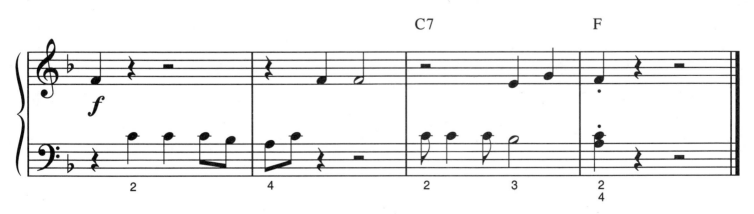

BOYS AND GIRLS COME OUT TO PLAY

TRADITIONAL
Arranged by DAN COATES

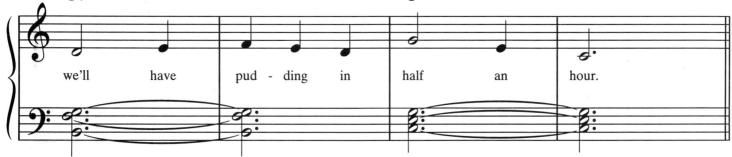

COCKLES AND MUSSELS

TRADITIONAL
Arranged by DAN COATES

Chorus:

live, a - live - oh.___ A - live, a - live - oh.___ Cry - ing,

"Cock-les and mus-sels, a - live, a - live - oh." 2. She
3. She

oh." A -

live, a - live - oh.___ A - live, a - live - oh.___ Cry - ing,

"Cock - les and mus - sels, a - live, a - live - oh."

Verse 2:
She was a fishmonger, and that the wonder,
Her father and mother were fishmongers too.
They drove wheelbarrows
Through streets broad and narrow,
Crying, "Cockles and mussels, alive, alive-oh."
(To Chorus:)

Verse 3:
She died of the fever and nothing could save her,
And that was the end of Sweet Molly Malone.
But her ghost drives the barrow
Through streets broad and narrow,
Crying, "Cockles and mussels, alive, alive-oh."
(To Chorus:)

BYE BABY BUNTING

TRADITIONAL
Arranged by DAN COATES

DO YOU KEN JOHN PEEL?

TRADITIONAL
Arranged by DAN COATES

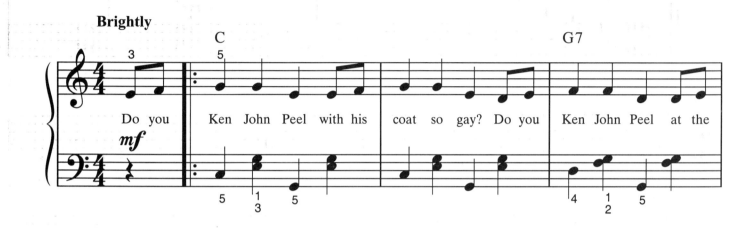

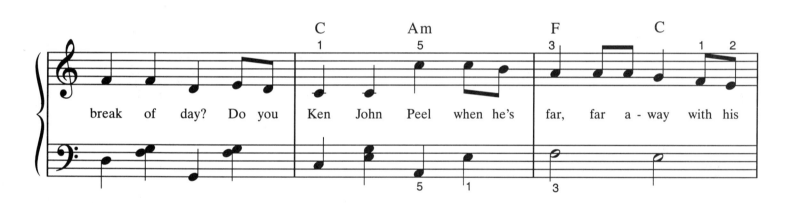

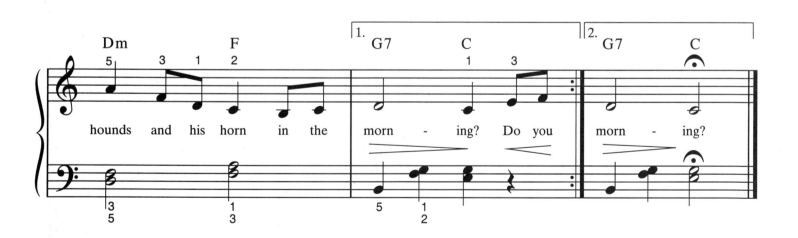

0578B

DADDY WOULDN'T BUY ME A BOW-WOW

TRADITIONAL
Arranged by DAN COATES

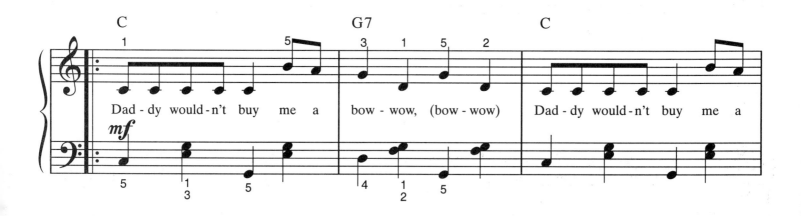

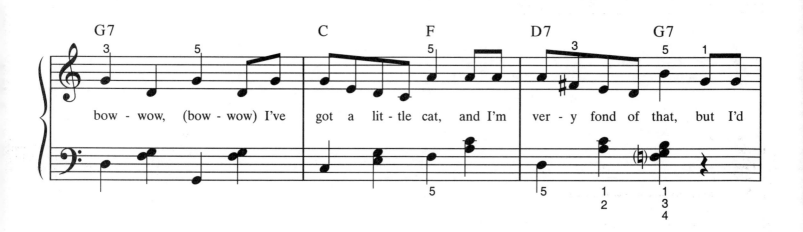

Daddy Wouldn't Buy Me a Bow-Wow - 2 - 1
0578B

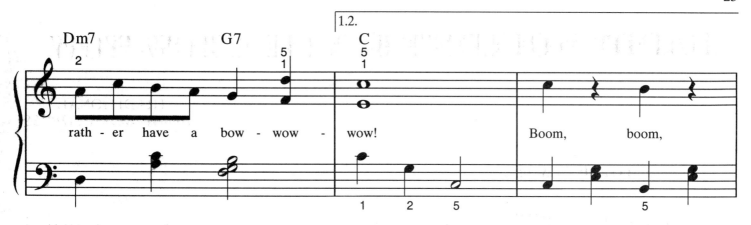

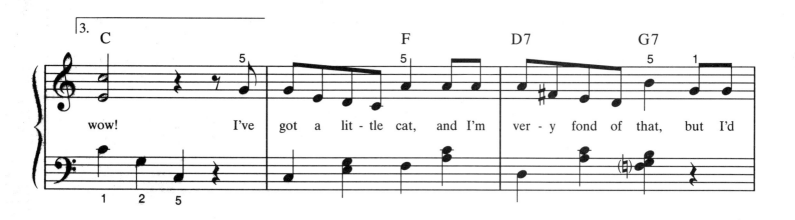

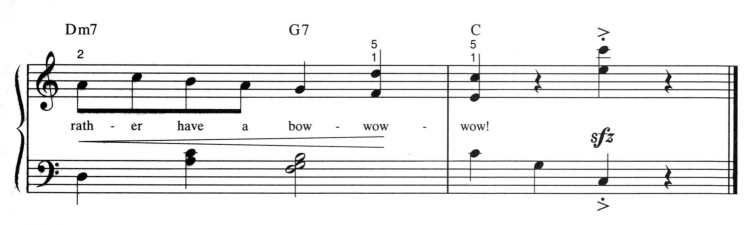

DAISY, DAISY
(BICYCLE BUILT FOR TWO)

Words and Music by
HARRY DACRE
Arranged by DAN COATES

Bright waltz

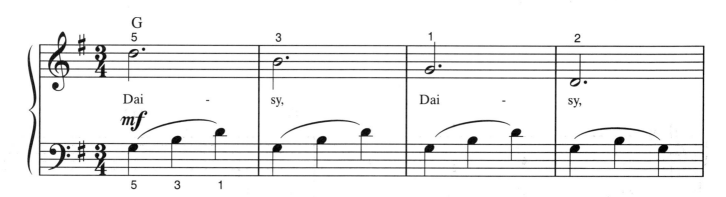

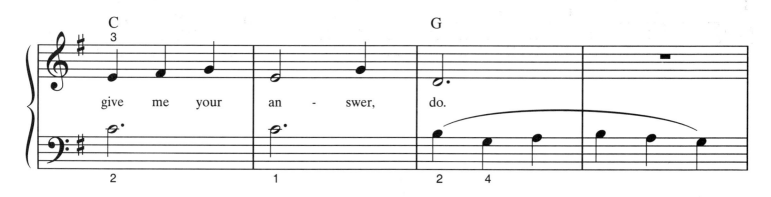

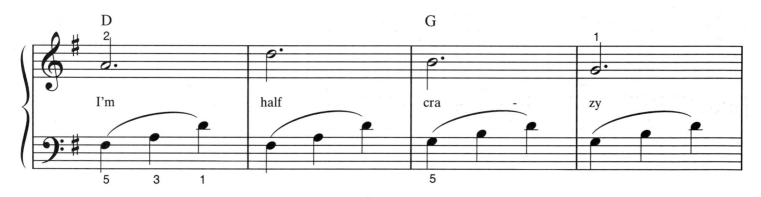

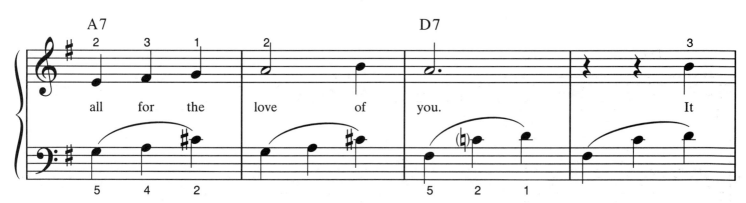

Daisy, Daisy - 2 - 1
0578B

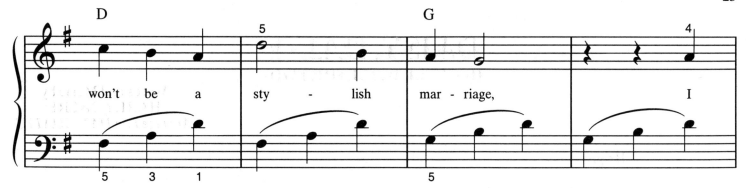

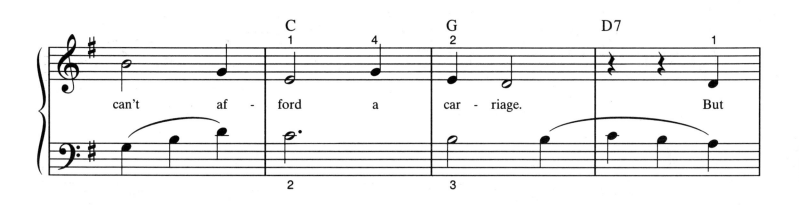

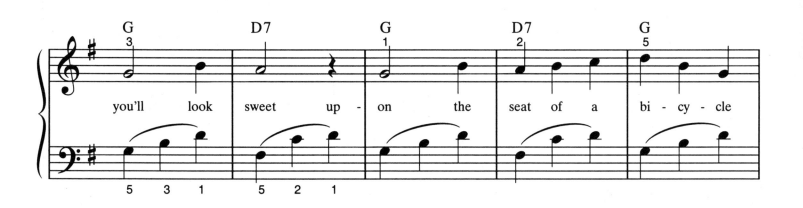

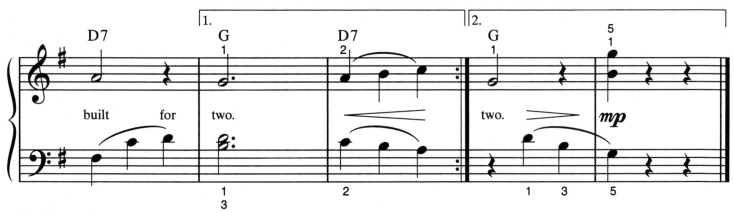

DO YOUR EARS HANG LOW?

TRADITIONAL
Arranged by DAN COATES

Not too fast

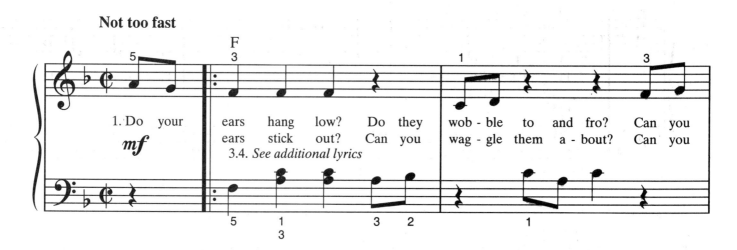

1. Do your ears hang low? Do they wob-ble to and fro? Can you
   ears stick out? Can you wag-gle them a-bout? Can you
   3.4. *See additional lyrics*

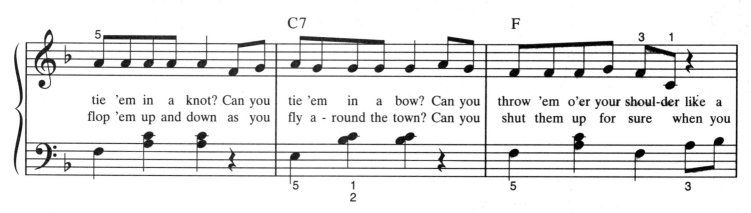

tie 'em in a knot? Can you tie 'em in a bow? Can you throw 'em o'er your shoul-der like a
flop 'em up and down as you fly a-round the town? Can you shut them up for sure when you

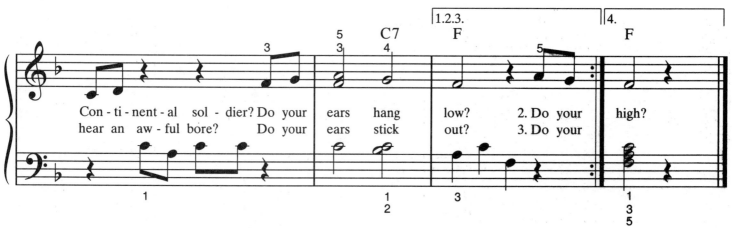

Con-ti-nent-al sol-dier? Do your ears hang low? 2. Do your
hear an aw-ful bore? Do your ears stick out? 3. Do your high?

Verse 3:
Do your ears flip-flop?
Can you use 'em as a mop?
Are they stringy at the bottom?
Are they curly at the top?
Can you use 'em for a swatter?
Can you use 'em for a blotter?
Do your ears flip-flop?

Verse 4:
Do your ears stand high?
Do they reach up to the sky?
Do they hang down when they're wet?
Do they stand up when they're dry?
Can you semaphore your neighbor
With a minimum of labor?
Do your ears stand high?

FIVE GREEN BOTTLES

TRADITIONAL
Arranged by DAN COATES

Verse 2:
Four green bottles hanging on the wall.
Four green bottles hanging on the wall.
And if one green bottle should accidently fall,
There'd be three green bottles hanging on the wall.

Verse 3:
Three green bottles hanging on the wall.
Three green bottles hanging on the wall.
And if one green bottle should accidently fall,
There'd be two green bottles hanging on the wall.

Verse 4:
Two green bottles hanging on the wall.
Two green bottles hanging on the wall.
And if one green bottle should accidently fall,
There'd be one green bottle hanging on the wall.

Verse 5:
One green bottle hanging on the wall.
One green bottle hanging on the wall.
And if one green bottle should accidently fall,
There'd be no green bottles hanging on the wall.

0578B

THE FARMER IN THE DELL

TRADITIONAL
Arranged by DAN COATES

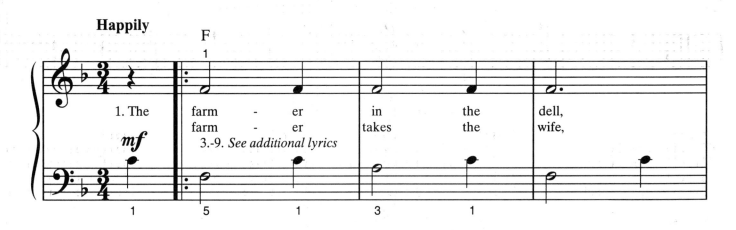

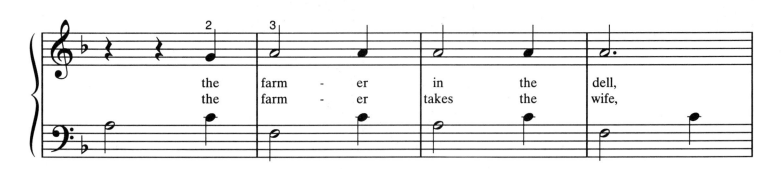

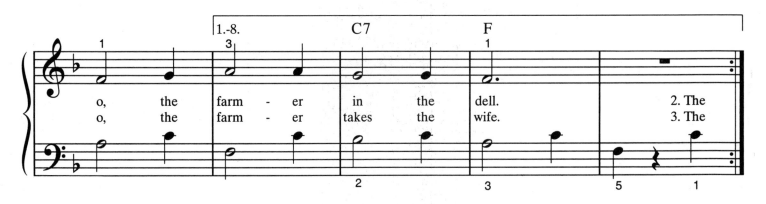

The Farmer in the Dell - 2 - 1
0578B

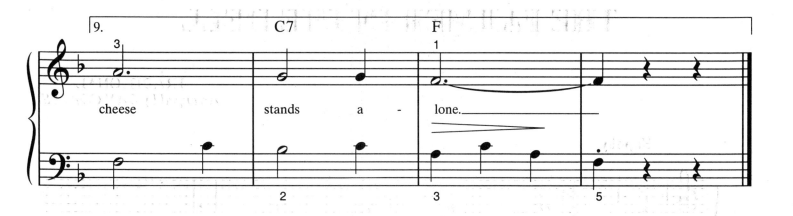

9.   C7   F

cheese   stands   a -   lone.

Verse 3:
The wife takes the child,
The wife takes the child,
Hi-ho the dairy-o,
The wife takes the child.

Verse 4:
The child takes the nurse,
The child takes the nurse,
Hi-ho the dairy-o,
The child takes the nurse.

Verse 5:
The nurse takes the dog,
The nurse takes the dog,
Hi-ho the dairy-o,
The nurse takes the dog.

Verse 6:
The dog takes the cat,
The dog takes the cat,
Hi-ho the dairy-o,
The dog takes the cat.

Verse 7:
The cat takes the rat,
The cat takes the rat,
Hi-ho the dairy-o,
The cat takes the rat.

Verse 8:
The rat takes the cheese,
The rat takes the cheese,
Hi-ho the dairy-o,
The rat takes the cheese.

Verse 9:
The cheese stands alone,
The cheese stands alone,
Hi-ho the dairy-o,
The cheese stands alone.

The Farmer in the Dell - 2 - 2
0578B

FOR HE'S A JOLLY-GOOD FELLOW

TRADITIONAL
Arranged by DAN COATES

Bright, steady beat

THE GRAND OLDE DUKE OF YORK

TRADITIONAL
Arranged by DAN COATES

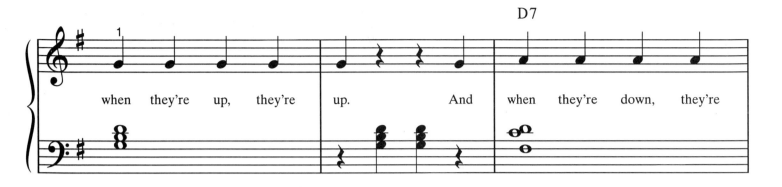

when they're up, they're up. And when they're down, they're

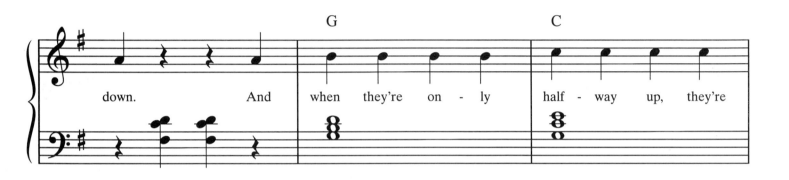

down. And when they're on - ly half - way up, they're

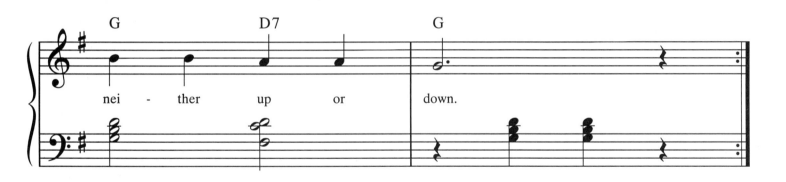

nei - ther up or down.

THE GRANDFATHER CLOCK

HENRY WORK
Arranged by DAN COATES

THE HAPPY WANDERER
(Val-De-Ri Val-De-Ra)

Words and Music by
FRIEDRICH W. MOLLER
and **ANTONIA RIDGE**
Arranged by DAN COATES

Moderate, steady beat

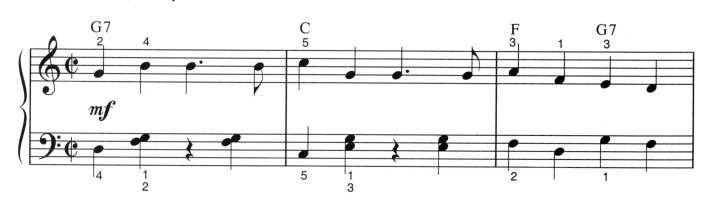

Verse:

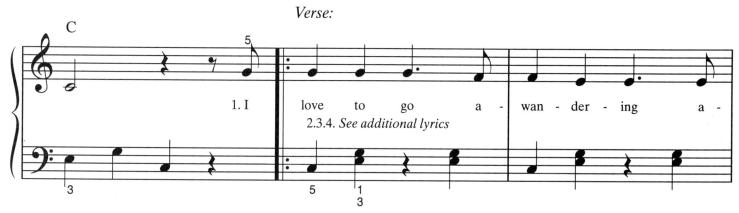

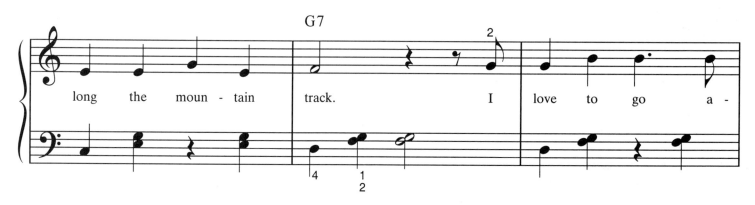

Chorus:

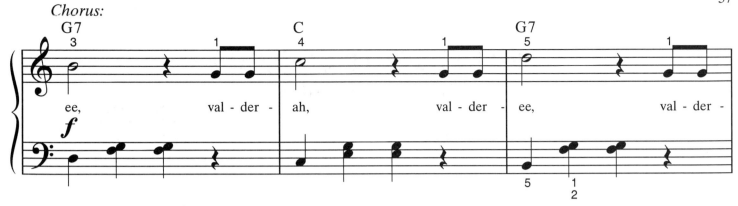

ee,   val - der - ah,   val - der - ee,   val - der -

ah - ha - ha - ha - ha - ha.   Val - der - ee,   val - der - ah,   my

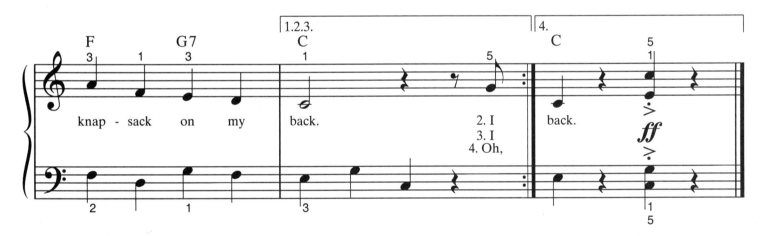

knap - sack   on   my   back.   back.

2. I
3. I
4. Oh,

Verse 2:
I love to wander by the stream
That dances in the sun.
So joyously, it calls to me,
"Come join my happy song."
(To Chorus:)

Verse 3:
I wave my hand to all I meet,
And they wave back to me.
And blackbirds call, so loud and sweet,
From every wooded tree.
 (To Chorus:)

Verse 4:
Oh, may I go awandering
Until the day I die.
Oh, may I always laugh and sing
Beneath God's dear blue sky.
(To Chorus:)

HAPPY BIRTHDAY

Words and Music by
MILDRED J. HILL and PATTY S. HILL
Arranged by DAN COATES

HERE WE GO LOOBY-LOO

TRADITIONAL
Arranged by DAN COATES

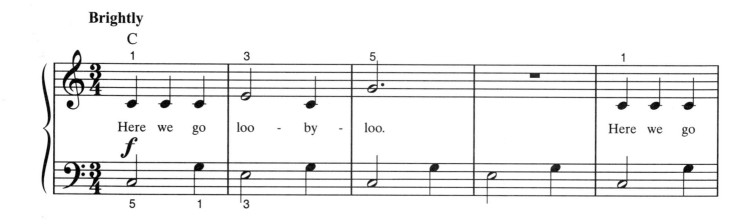

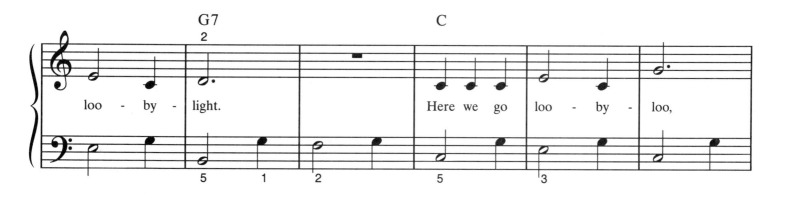

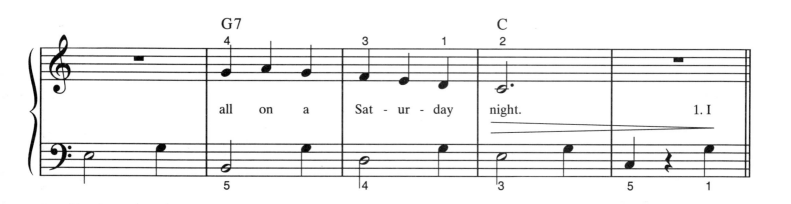

Here We Go Looby-Loo - 3 - 1
0578B

Verse:

put my right hand in.

2.3.4.5. *See additional lyrics*

mf

I take my

right hand out.

I give my hand a shake, shake,

G7   C

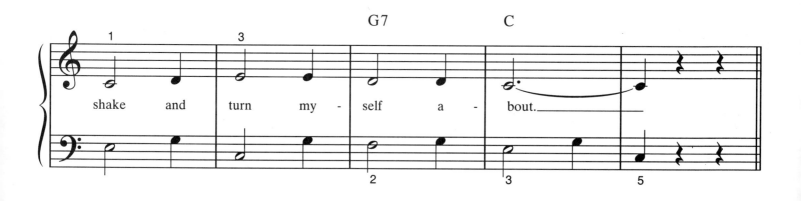

shake and turn my - self a - bout.____

Chorus:

Here we go loo - by - loo.

Here we go

f

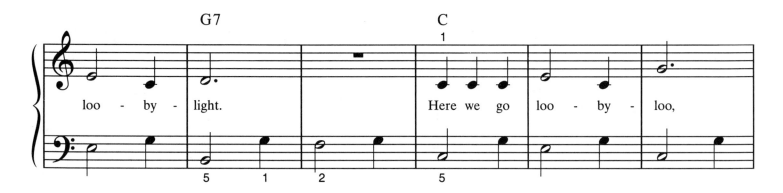

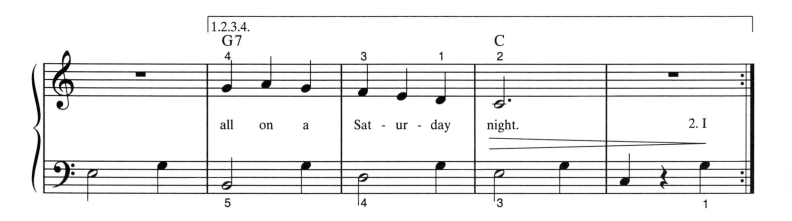

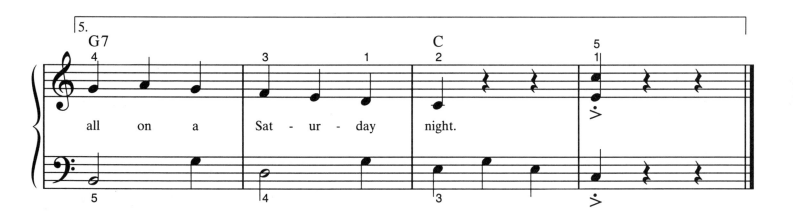

Verse 2:
I put my left hand in.
I take my left hand out.
I give my hand a shake, shake, shake
And turn myself about.
(To Chorus:)

Verse 3:
I put my right foot in.
I take my right foot out.
I give my foot a shake, shake, shake
And turn myself about.
(To Chorus:)

Verse 4:
I put my left foot in.
I take my left foot out.
I give my foot a shake, shake, shake
And turn myself about.
(To Chorus:)

Verse 5:
I put my whole self in.
I take my whole self out.
I give myself a shake, shake, shake
And turn myself about.
(To Chorus:)

HERE WE GO 'ROUND THE MULBERRY BUSH

TRADITIONAL
Arranged by DAN COATES

Bright and happy

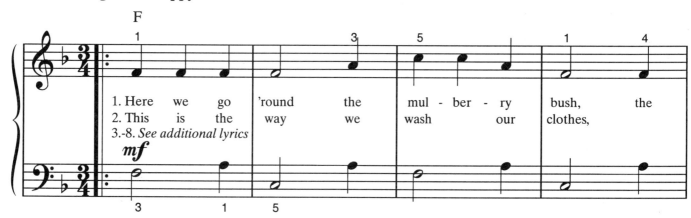

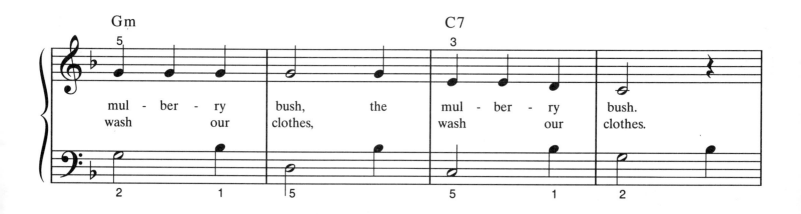

Here We Go 'Round the Mulberry Bush - 2 - 1
0578B

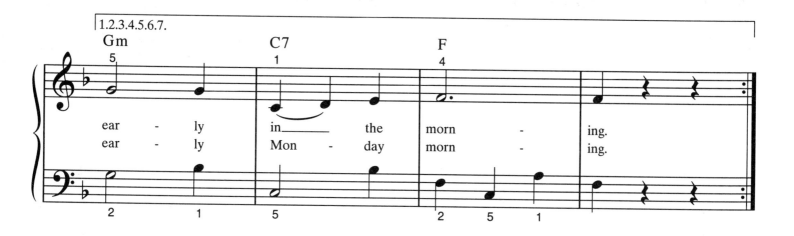

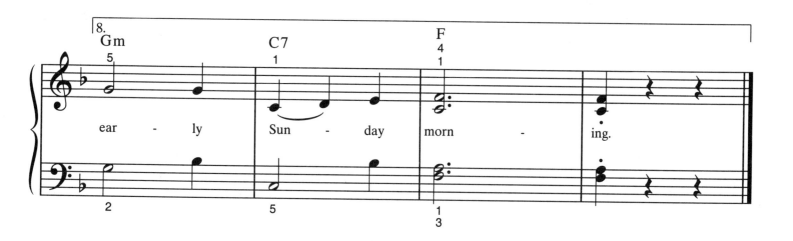

Verse 3:
This is the way we iron our clothes,
Iron our clothes, iron our clothes.
This is the way we iron our clothes
So early Tuesday morning.

Verse 4:
This is the way we mend our clothes,
Mend our clothes, mend our clothes.
This is the way we mend our clothes
So early Wednesday morning.

Verse 5:
This is the way we scrub the floor,
Scrub the floor, scrub the floor.
This is the way we scrub the floor
So early Thursday morning.

Verse 6:
This is the way we sweep the house,
Sweep the house, sweep the house.
This is the way we sweep the house
So early Friday morning.

Verse 7:
This is the way we bake our bread,
Bake our bread, bake our bread.
This is the way we bake our bread
So early Saturday morning.

Verse 8:
This is the way we go to church,
Go to church, go to church.
This is the way we go to church
So early Sunday morning.

HOME ON THE RANGE

TRADITIONAL
Arranged by DAN COATES

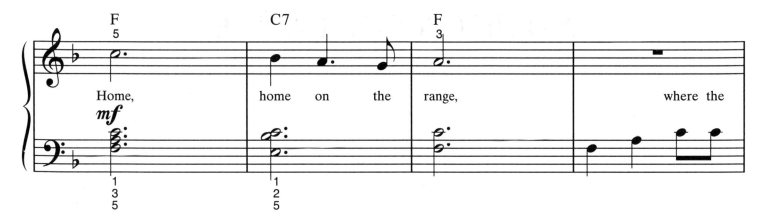

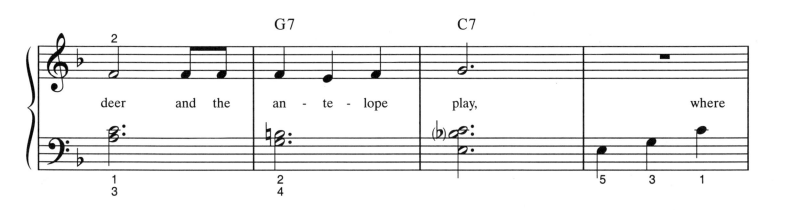

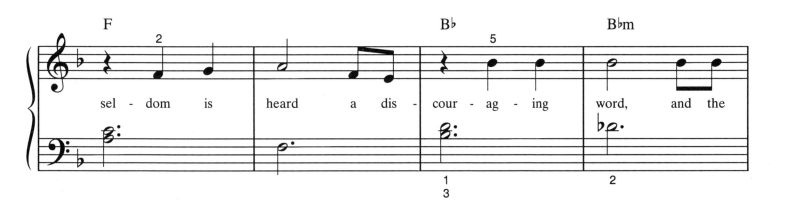

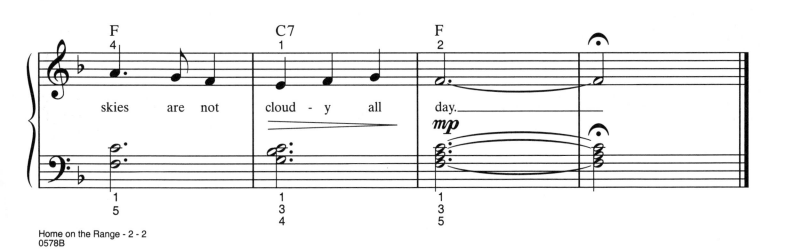

HICKORY DICKORY DOCK

TRADITIONAL
Arranged by DAN COATES

HOT CROSS BUNS

TRADITIONAL
Arranged by DAN COATES

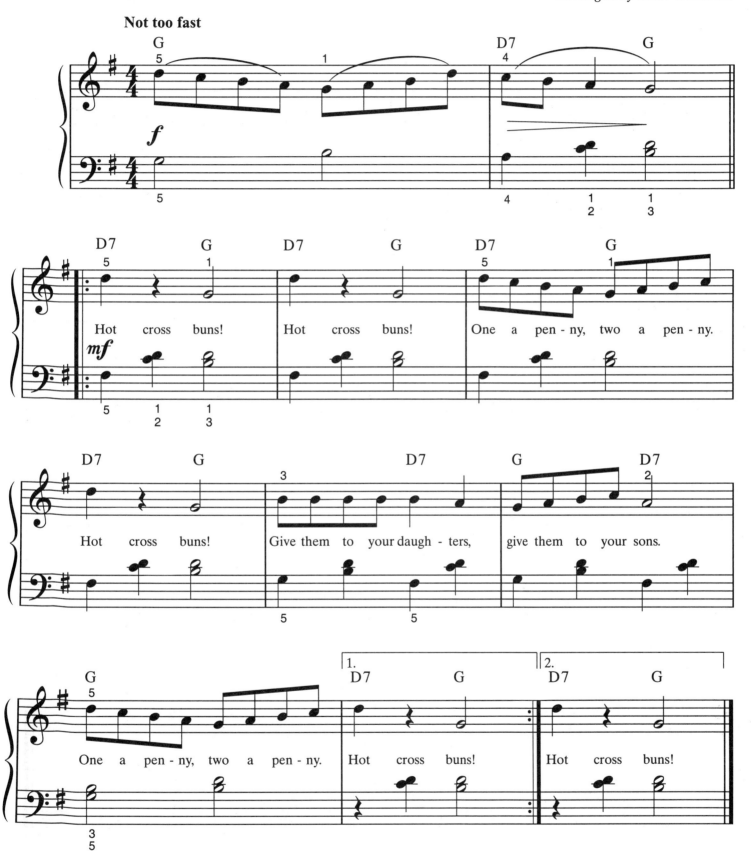

0578B

HOW MANY MILES TO BABYLON?

TRADITIONAL
Arranged by DAN COATES

HOW MUCH IS THAT DOGGIE IN THE WINDOW?

Words and Music by
BOB MERRILL
Arranged by DAN COATES

0578B

HUMPTY DUMPTY

TRADITIONAL
Arranged by DAN COATES

HUSH LITTLE BABY

TRADITIONAL
Arranged by DAN COATES

Verse 3:
If that billy goat won't pull,
Papa's gonna buy you a cart and bull.
If that cart and bull turns over,
Papa's gonna buy you a dog named Rover.

Verse 4:
If that dog named Rover won't bark,
Papa's gonna buy you a horse and cart.
If that horse and cart fall down,
You'll still be the sweetest baby in town.

I HAD A LITTLE NUT TREE

TRADITIONAL
Arranged by DAN COATES

Moderate, walking tempo

I had a lit - tle nut tree, noth-ing would it bear, but a sil - ver nut - meg

and a gold-en pear. The king of Spain's_ daugh - ter came to vis - it me, and

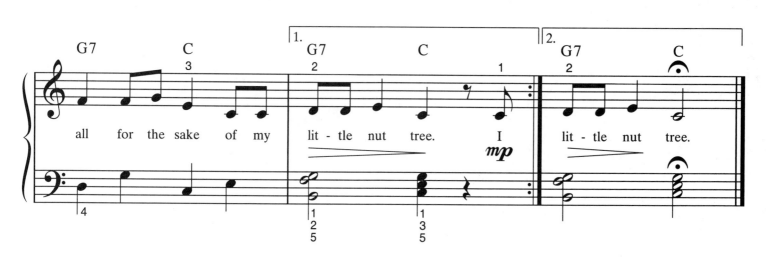

all for the sake of my lit - tle nut tree. I lit - tle nut tree.

I SAW THREE SHIPS

TRADITIONAL
Arranged by DAN COATES

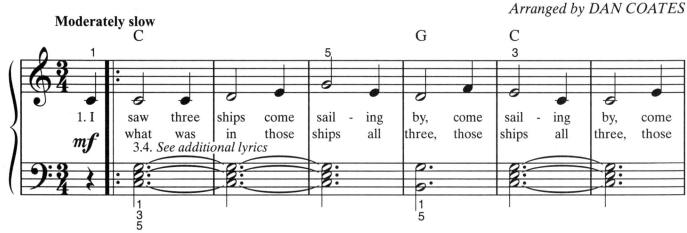

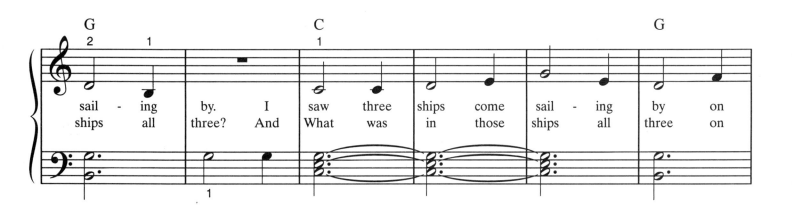

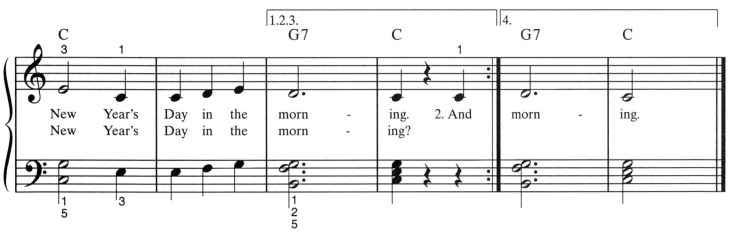

Verse 3:
Three pretty girls were in all three,
Were in all three, were in all three.
Three pretty girls were in all three
On New Year's Day in the morning.

Verse 4:
One could whistle and one could sing,
And one could play on the violin.
The joy there was at my wedding
On New Year's Day in the morning.

I'VE BEEN WORKING ON THE RAILROAD

TRADITIONAL
Arranged by DAN COATES

Bright and happy

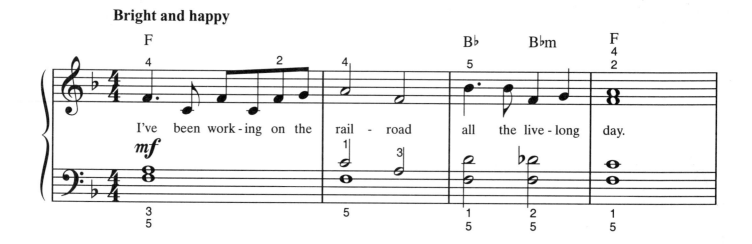

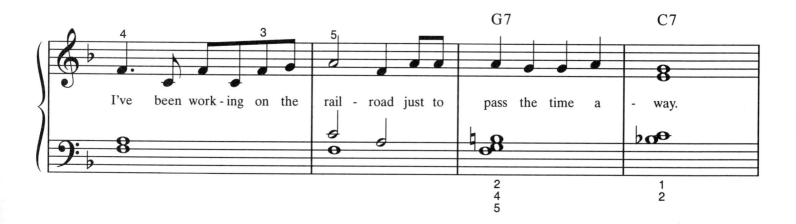

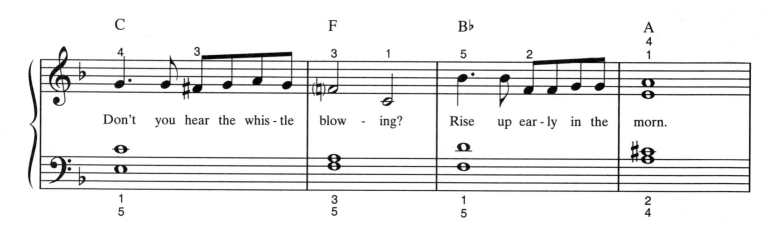

I've Been Working on the Railroad - 2 - 1
0578B

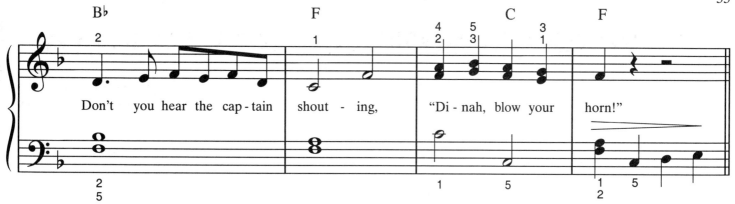

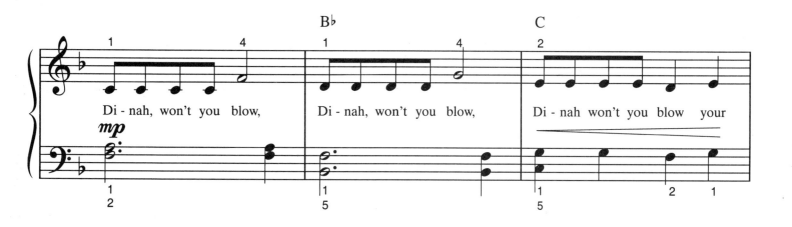

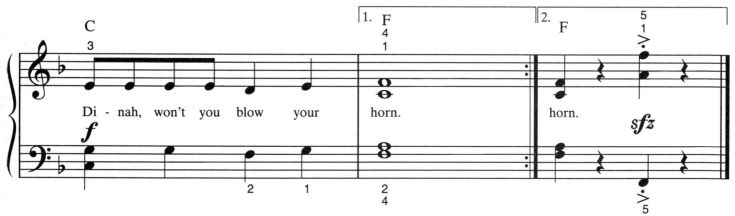

I'M H-A-P-P-Y!

TRADITIONAL
Arranged by DAN COATES

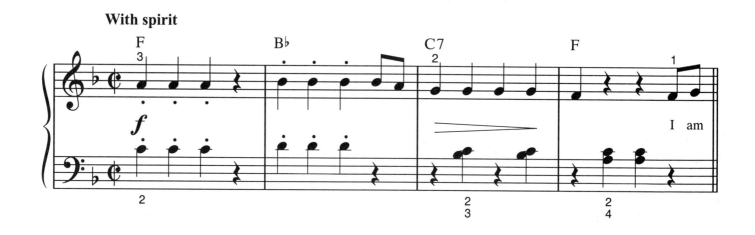

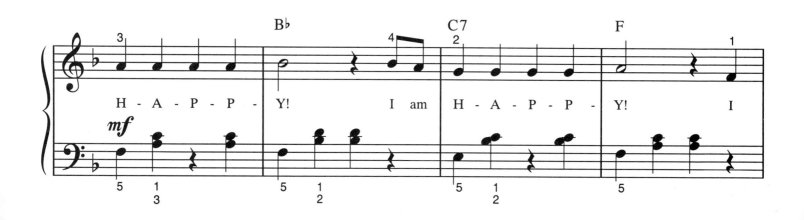

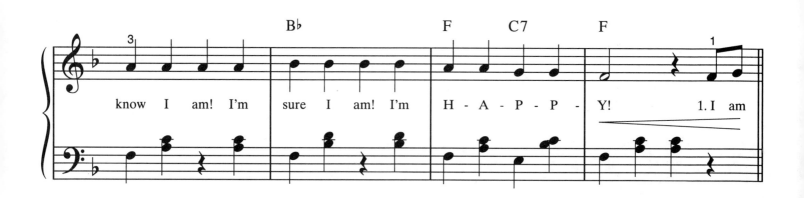

I'm H-A-P-P-Y! - 2 - 1
0578B

57

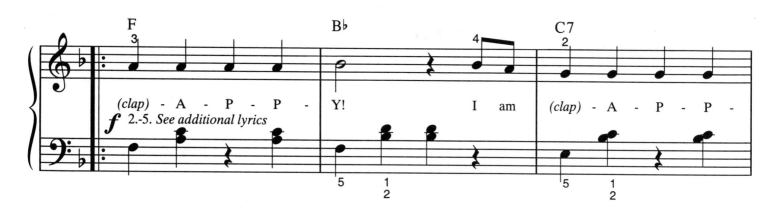

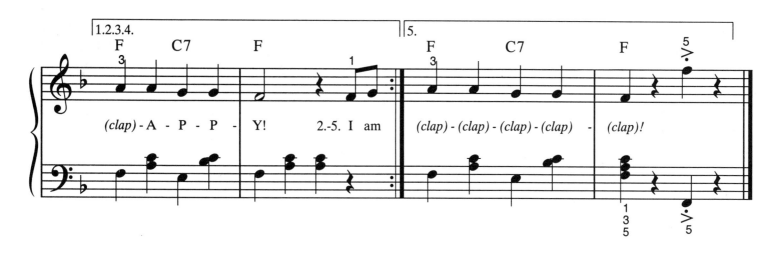

Verse 2:
I am *(clap)-(clap)*-P-P-Y!
I am *(clap)-(clap)*-P-P-Y!
I know I am!
I'm sure I am!
I'm *(clap)-(clap)*-P-P-Y!

Verse 3:
I am *(clap-(clap)-(clap)*-P-Y!
I am *(clap-(clap)-(clap)*-P-Y!
I know I am!
I'm sure I am!
I'm *(clap-(clap)-(clap)*-P-Y!

Verse 4:
I am *(clap)-(clap)-(clap)-(clap)*-Y!
I am *(clap)-(clap)-(clap)-(clap)*-Y!
I know I am!
I'm sure I am!
I'm *(clap)-(clap)-(clap)-(clap)*-Y!

Verse 5:
I am *(clap)-(clap)-(clap)-(clap)-(clap)!*
I am *(clap)-(clap)-(clap)-(clap)-(clap)!*
I know I am!
I'm sure I am!
I'm *(clap)-(clap)-(clap)-(clap)-(clap)!*

I'm H-A-P-P-Y! - 2 - 2
0578B

I'M A LITTLE TEAPOT

TRADITIONAL
Arranged by DAN COATES

Happily

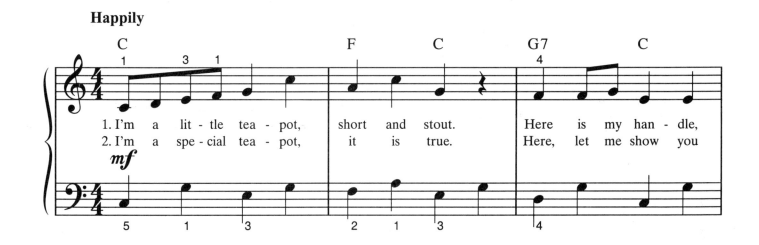

1. I'm a lit - tle tea - pot, short and stout. Here is my han - dle,
2. I'm a spe - cial tea - pot, it is true. Here, let me show you

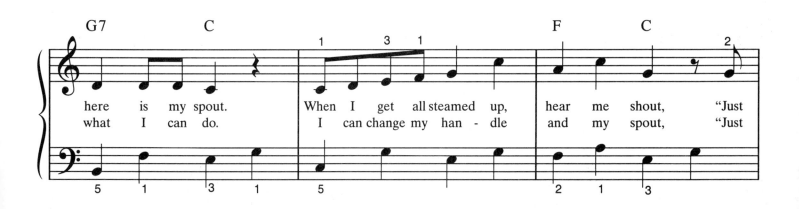

here is my spout. When I get all steamed up, hear me shout, "Just
what I can do. I can change my han - dle and my spout, "Just

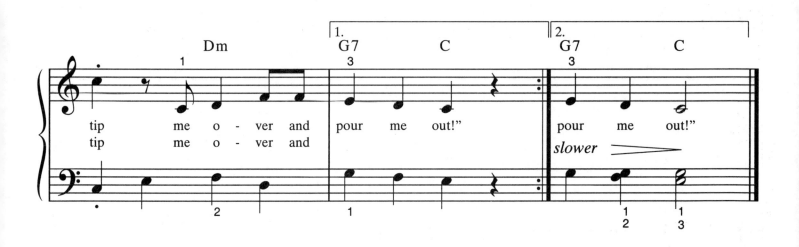

tip me o - ver and pour me out!" pour me out!"
tip me o - ver and *slower*

A-TISKET, A-TASKET

TRADITIONAL
Arranged by DAN COATES

0578B

INCY-WINCY SPIDER

TRADITIONAL
Arranged by DAN COATES

Moderately slow

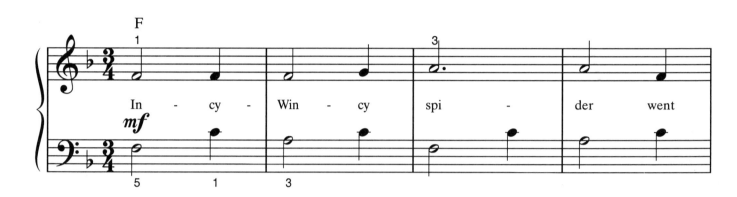

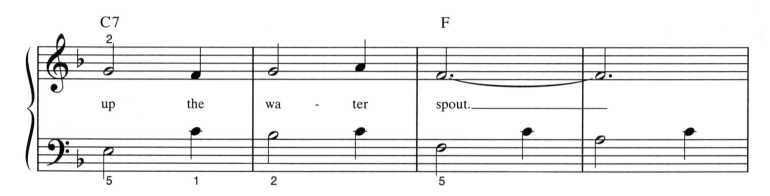

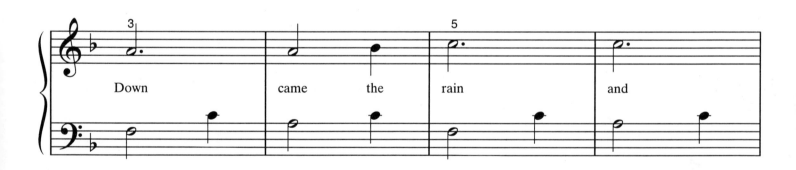

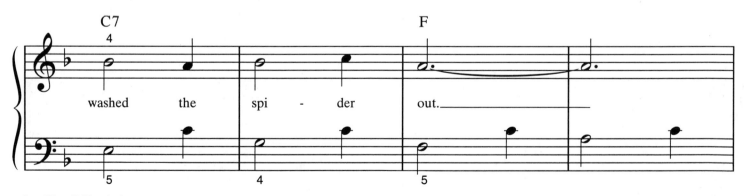

Incy-Wincy Spider - 2 - 1
0578B

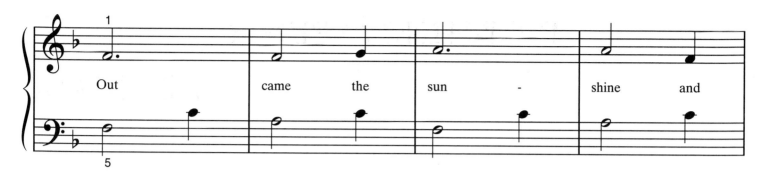

Out   came   the   sun - shine   and

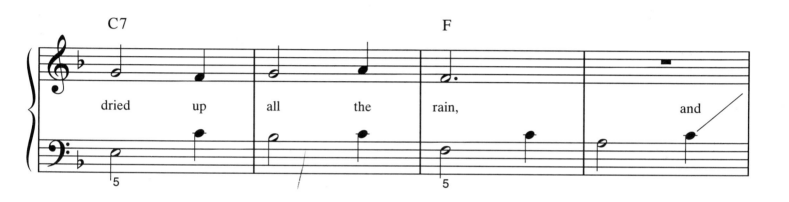

C7   F

dried   up   all   the   rain,   and

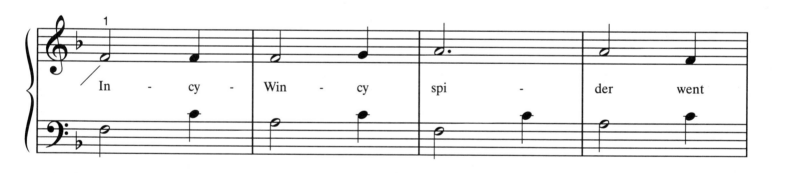

In - cy - Win - cy   spi - der   went

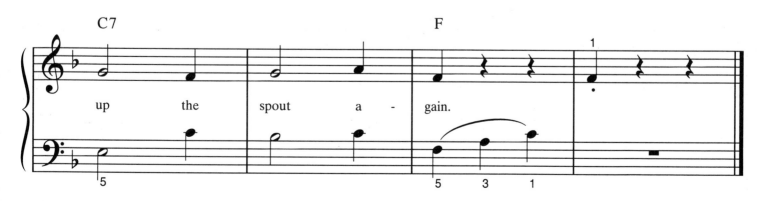

C7   F

up   the   spout   a - gain.

JACK AND JILL

TRADITIONAL
Arranged by DAN COATES

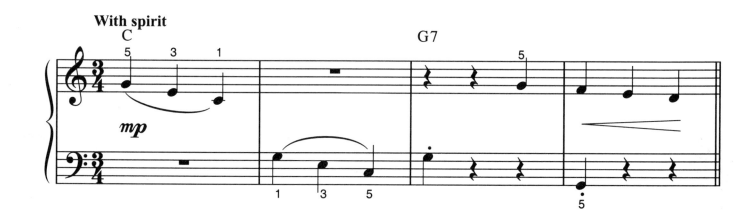

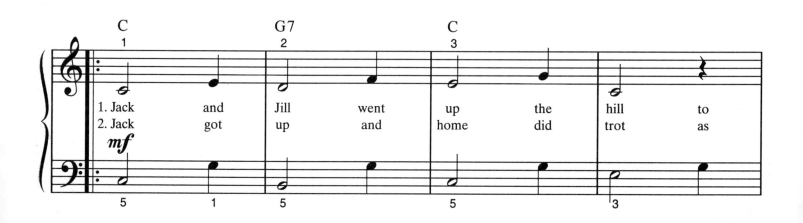

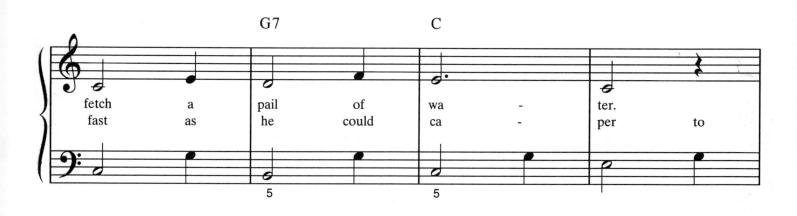

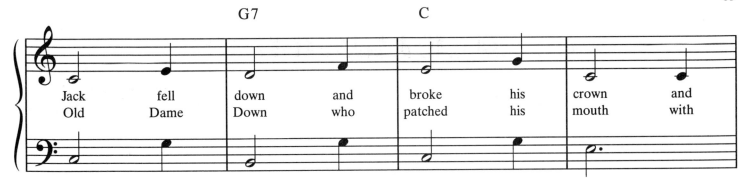

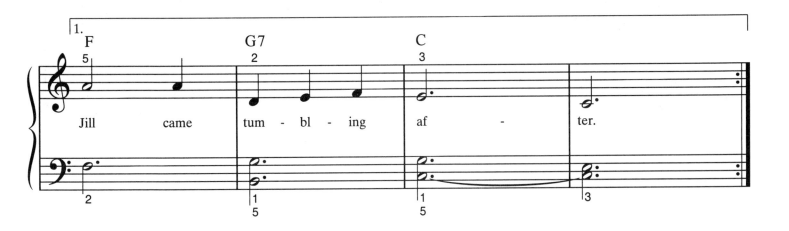

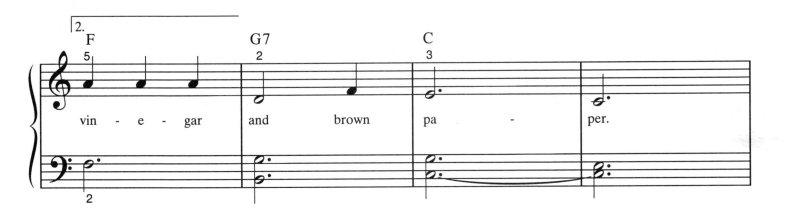

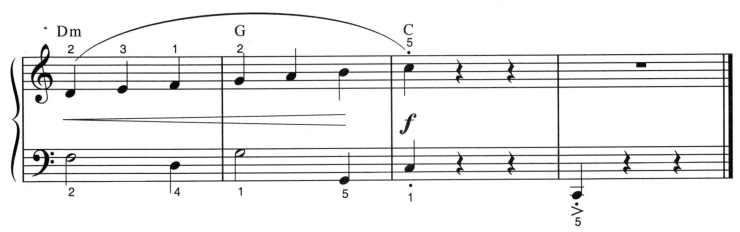

COCK-A-DOODLE-DOO!

TRADITIONAL
Arranged by DAN COATES

Brightly

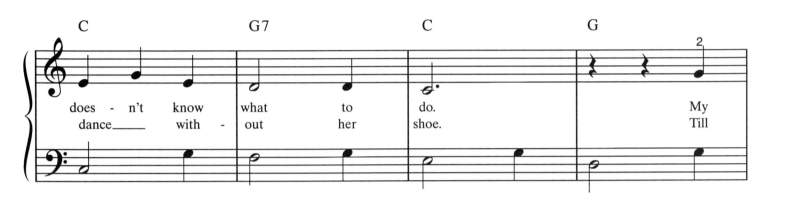

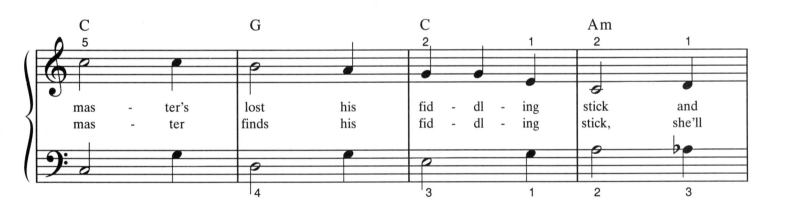

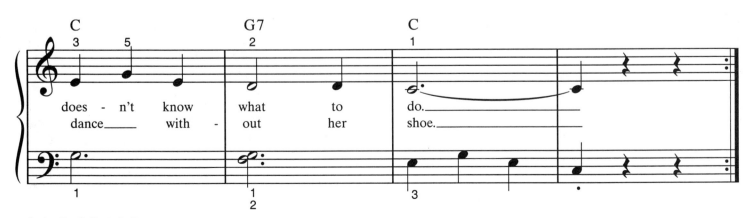

HEY DIDDLE DIDDLE

TRADITIONAL
Arranged by DAN COATES

JOHN BROWN'S BABY

TRADITIONAL
Arranged by DAN COATES

Moderately slow

John Brown's ba - by had a cold up - on its chest. John Brown's ba - by had a

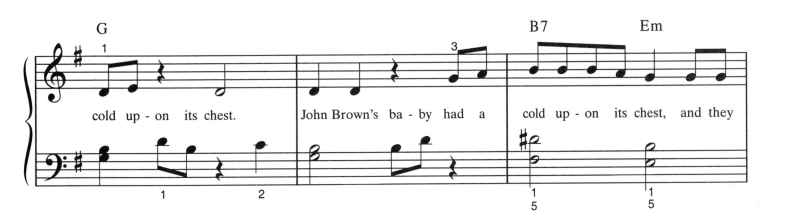

cold up - on its chest. John Brown's ba - by had a cold up - on its chest, and they

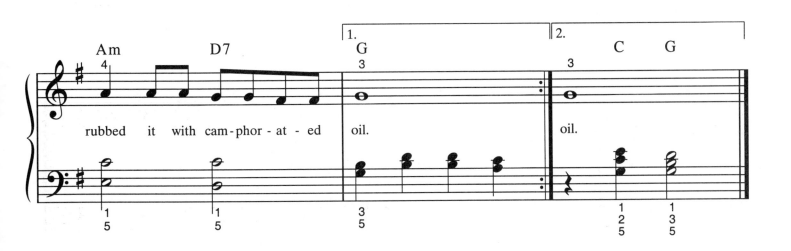

rubbed it with cam - phor - at - ed oil. oil.

0578B

LAVENDER'S BLUE

TRADITIONAL
Arranged by DAN COATES

Moderately slow waltz

LITTLE BOY BLUE

TRADITIONAL
Arranged by DAN COATES

0578B

LITTLE BO PEEP

TRADITIONAL
Arranged by DAN COATES

Little Bo Peep - 2 - 1
0578B

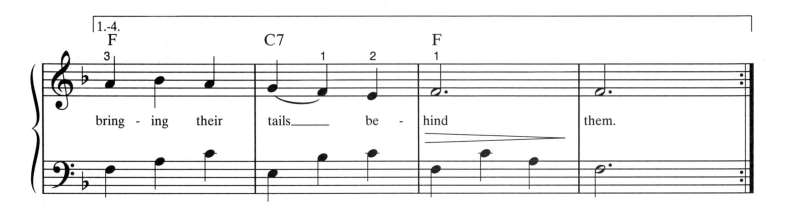

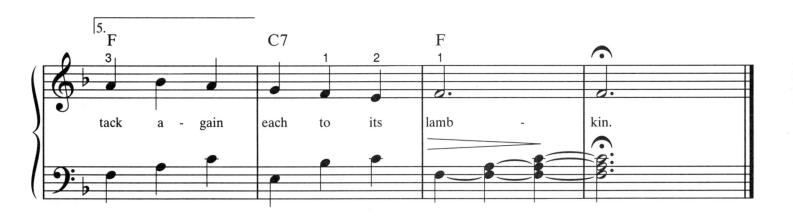

Verse 2:
Little Bo Peep fell fast asleep
And dreamed she heard them bleating.
And once she awoke, she found it a joke,
For they were still a fleeting.

Verse 3:
Then she took up her little crook,
Determined to find them.
She found them, indeed, it made her heart bleed,
For they left their tails behind them.

Verse 4:
It happened one day as Bo Peep did stray
Into a green meadow hard by.
There she espied their tails side by side,
All hung on a big tree to dry.

Verse 5:
She heaved a sigh and wiped her eye
And over the hillocks went rambling.
She tried what she could as a shepherdess should
To tack again each to its lambkin.

LITTLE JACK HORNER

TRADITIONAL
Arranged by DAN COATES

LITTLE MISS MUFFET

TRADITIONAL
Arranged by DAN COATES

LONDON BRIDGE IS FALLING DOWN

TRADITIONAL
Arranged by DAN COATES

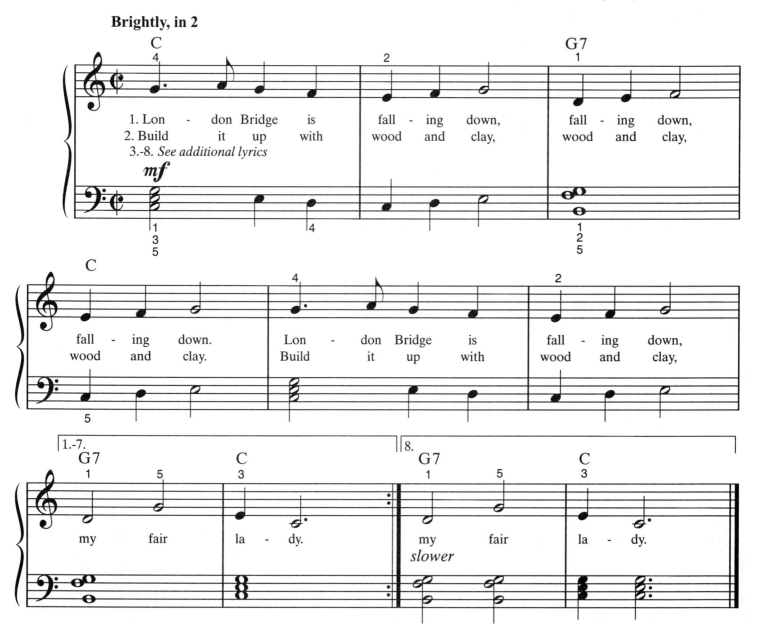

Verse 3:
Wood and clay will wash away,
Wash away, wash away.
Wood and clay will wash away,
My fair lady.

Verse 4:
Build it up with iron and steel,
Iron and steel, iron and steel.
Build it up with iron and steel,
My fair lady.

Verse 5:
Iron and steel will bend and bow,
Bend and bow, bend and bow.
Iron and steel will bend and bow,
My fair lady.

Verse 6:
Build it up with silver and gold,
Silver and gold, silver and gold.
Build it up with silver and gold,
My fair lady.

Verse 7:
Silver and gold will be stolen away,
Stolen away, stolen away.
Silver and gold will be stolen away,
My fair lady.

Verse 8:
Send two men to watch all night,
Watch all night, watch all night.
Send two men to watch all night,
My fair lady.

LONDON'S BURNING

TRADITIONAL
Arranged by DAN COATES

Note: Second time through,
may be sung as a round.
(Begin round at *)

0578B

LUCY LOCKET

TRADITIONAL
Arranged by DAN COATES

With a steady beat

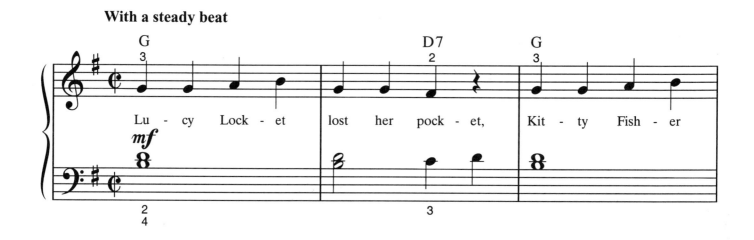

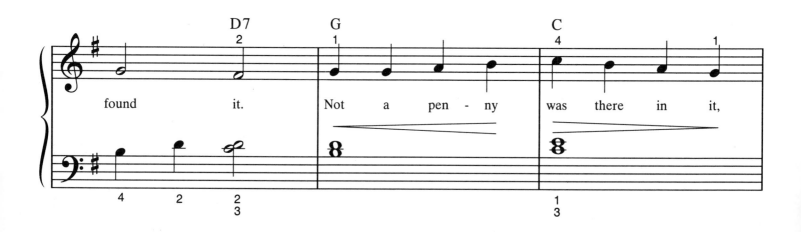

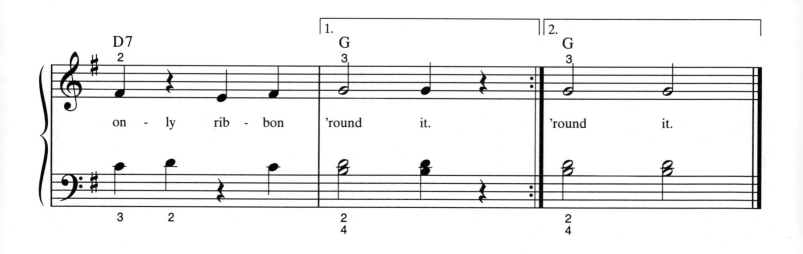

LULLABY AND GOODNIGHT

TRADITIONAL
Arranged by DAN COATES

Gentle waltz

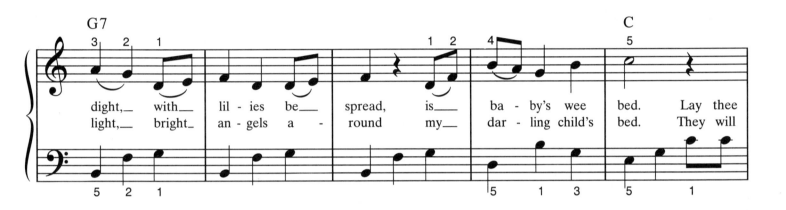

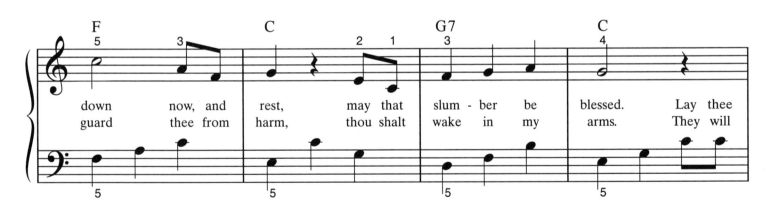

0578B

MARY HAD A LITTLE LAMB

TRADITIONAL
Arranged by DAN COATES

0578B

MICHAEL FINNIGAN

TRADITIONAL
Arranged by DAN COATES

Bright march tempo

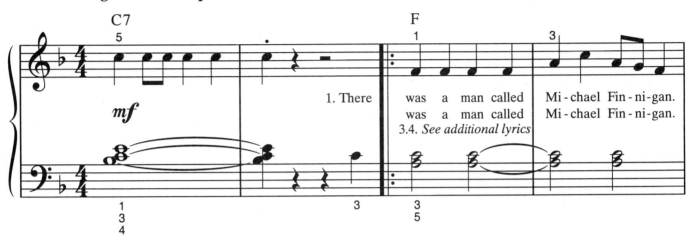

Verse 3:
There was a man called Michael Finnigan,
He went fishing with a pinnigan.
Caught a fish and dropped it in again.
Poor old Michael Finnigan!

Verse 4:
There was a man called Michael Finnigan,
He grew fat and then grew thin again.
Then he died and had to begin again.
Poor old Michael Finnigan!

THE MUFFIN MAN

TRADITIONAL
Arranged by DAN COATES

Happily

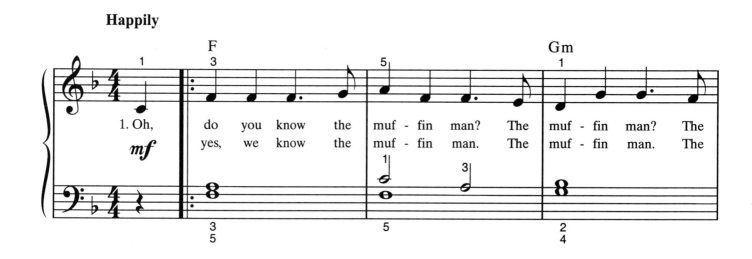

1. Oh, do you know the muf - fin man? The muf - fin man? The
   yes, we know the muf - fin man. The muf - fin man. The

muf - fin man? Oh, do you know the muf - fin man who
muf - fin man. Oh yes, we know the muf - fin man who

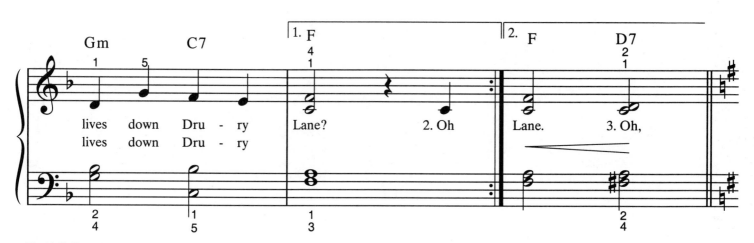

lives down Dru - ry Lane? 2. Oh Lane. 3. Oh,
lives down Dru - ry

The Muffin Man - 2 - 1
0578B

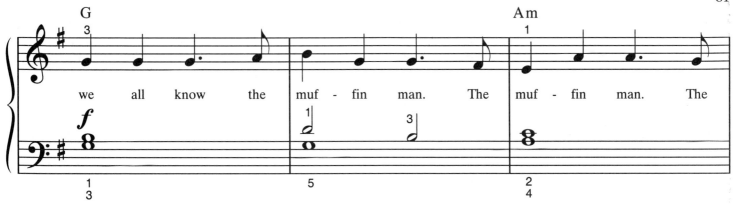

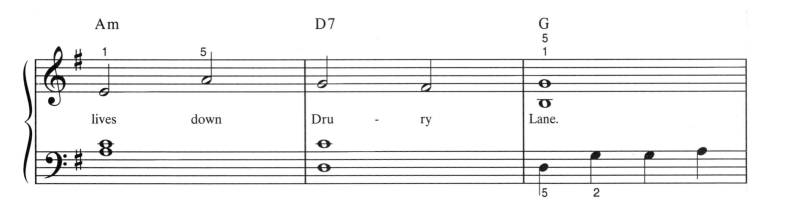

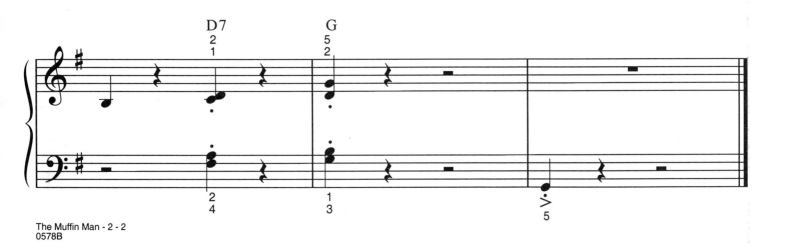

The Muffin Man - 2 - 2
0578B

MY BONNIE LIES OVER THE OCEAN

TRADITIONAL
Arranged by DAN COATES

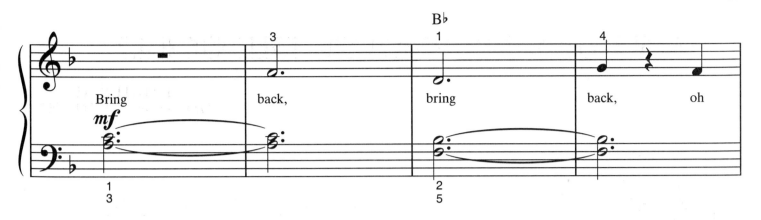

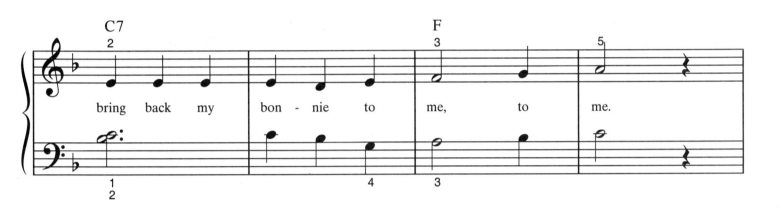

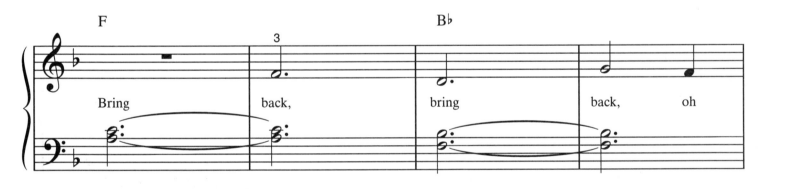

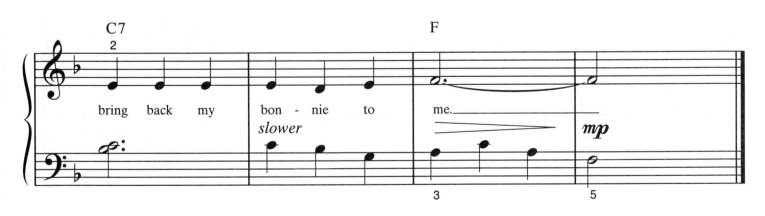

THE NORTH WIND DOTH BLOW

TRADITIONAL
Arranged by DAN COATES

OH DEAR, WHAT CAN THE MATTER BE?

TRADITIONAL
Arranged by DAN COATES

Oh, dear! What can the mat - ter be?

Oh, dear! What can the mat - ter be?

Oh, dear! What can the mat - ter be?

John - ny's so long at the fair. He

Oh Dear, What Can the Matter Be? - 3 - 1
0578B

prom - ised he'd buy me a bunch of blue rib - bons. He

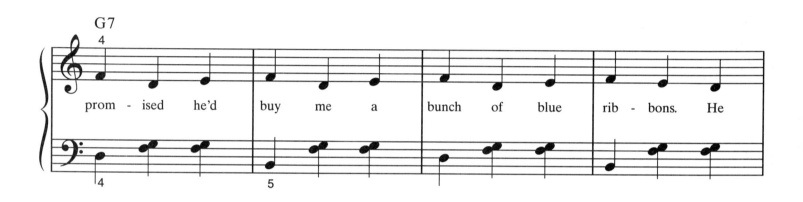

G7

prom - ised he'd buy me a bunch of blue rib - bons. He

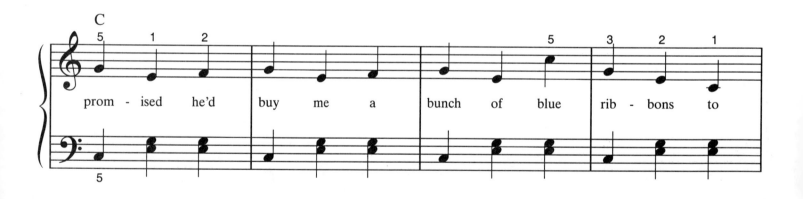

C

prom - ised he'd buy me a bunch of blue rib - bons to

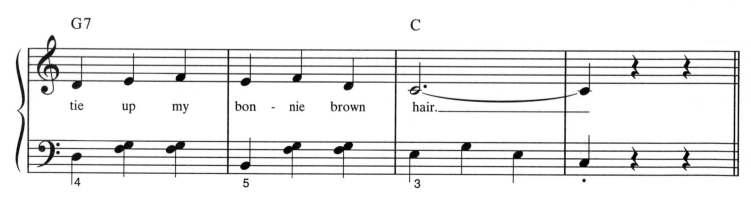

G7   C

tie up my bon - nie brown hair.

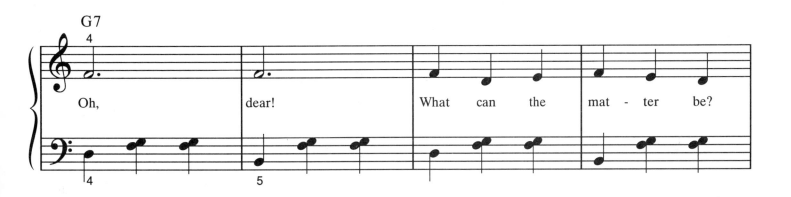

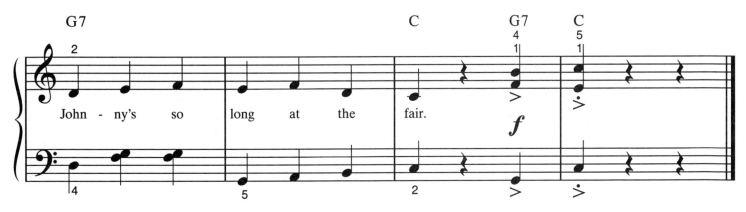

Oh Dear, What Can the Matter Be? - 3 - 3
0578B

OH WHERE, OH WHERE HAS MY LITTLE DOG GONE?

TRADITIONAL
Arranged by DAN COATES

Moderate waltz

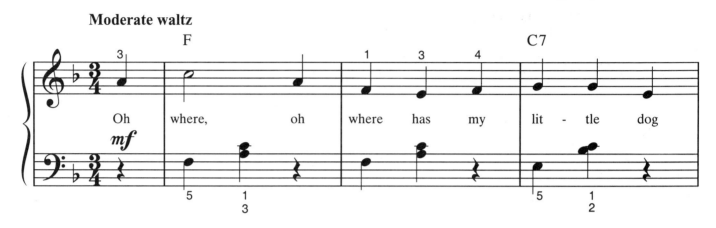

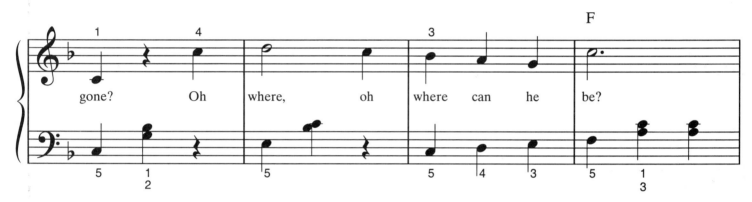

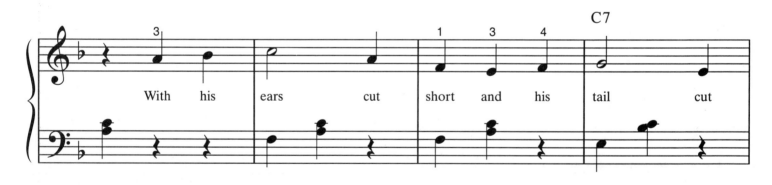

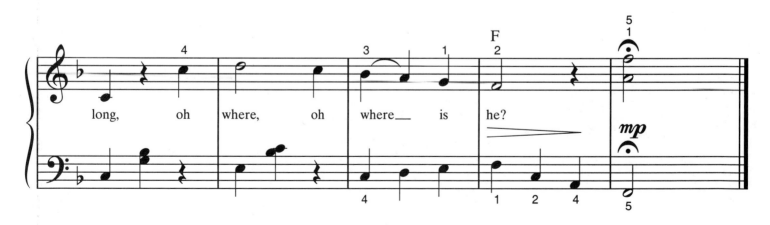

OLD MACDONALD HAD A FARM

TRADITIONAL
Arranged by DAN COATES

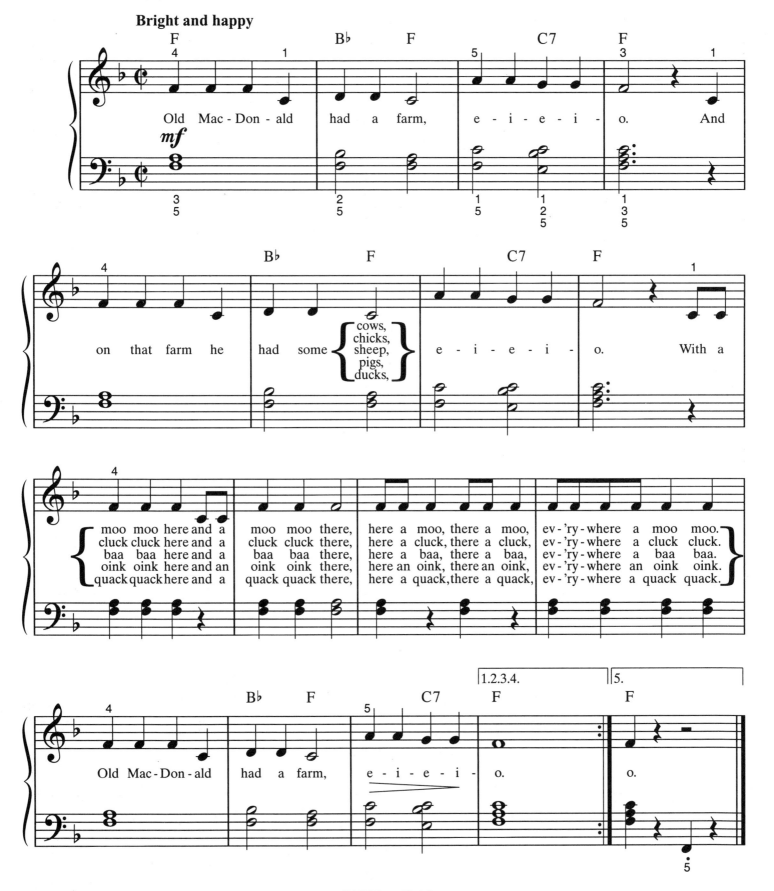

0578B

THE OLD GREY MARE

TRADITIONAL
Arranged by DAN COATES

go.   Oh, the   old grey mare, she   ain't what she used to be

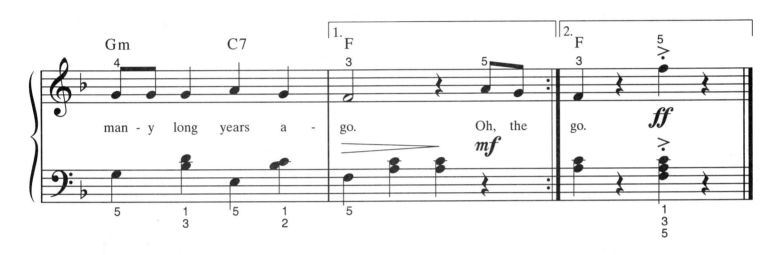

man - y   long   years   a -   go.   Oh, the   go.

ON TOP OF OLD SMOKEY

TRADITIONAL
Arranged by DAN COATES

Moderately slow waltz

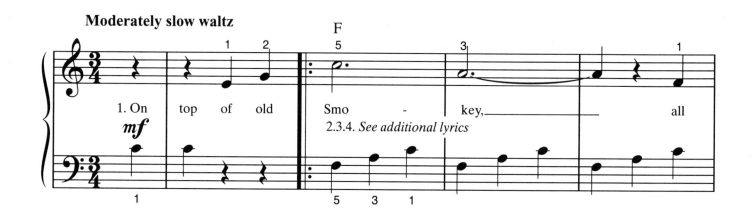

1. On top of old Smo - key,_____ all
2.3.4. *See additional lyrics*

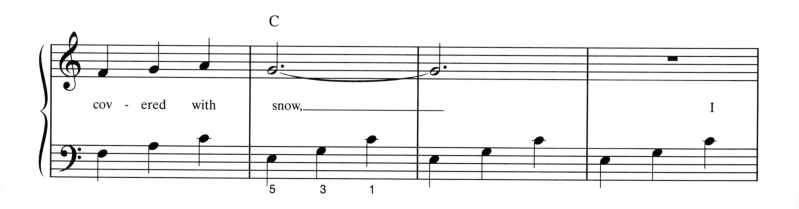

cov - ered with snow,_____ I

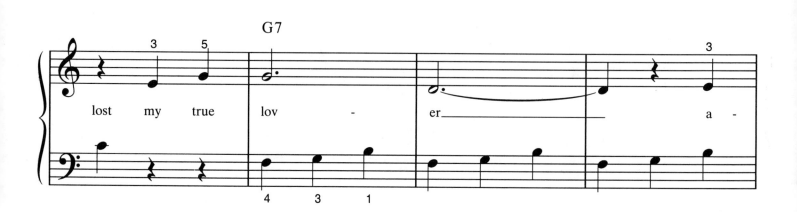

lost my true lov - er_____ a -

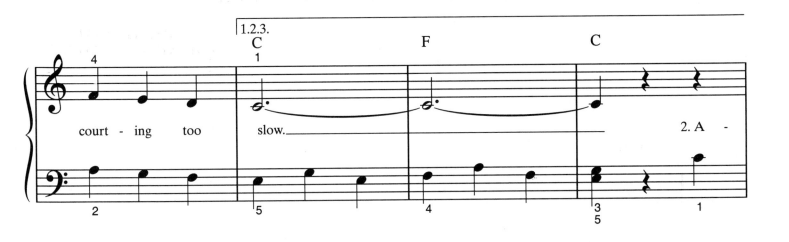

court - ing too slow.

F

C

2. A -

court - ing's a

slow.
rit.

F

C

mp

Verse 2:
Acourting's a pleasure,
And flirtings are brief.
A false-hearted lover
Is worse than a thief.

Verse 3:
She'll hug you and kiss you
And tell you more lies
Than the cross stars on the railroad
Or stars in the sky.

Verse 4:
On top of old Smokey,
All covered with snow,
I lost my true lover
Acourting too slow.

ONE MAN WENT TO MOW

TRADITIONAL
Arranged by DAN COATES

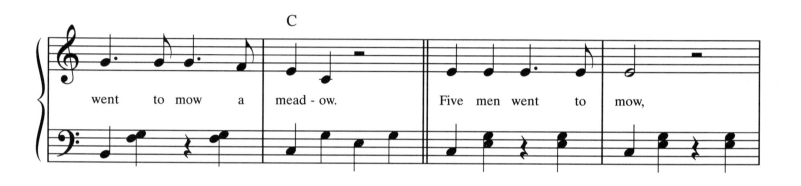

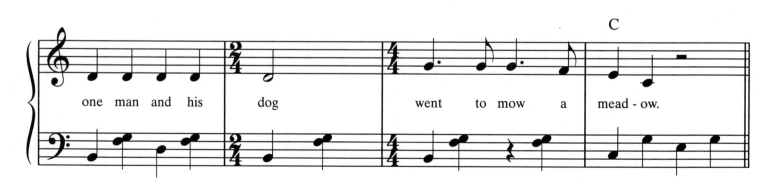

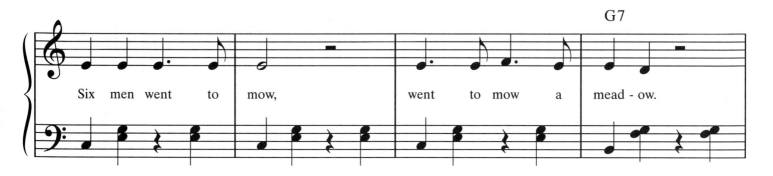

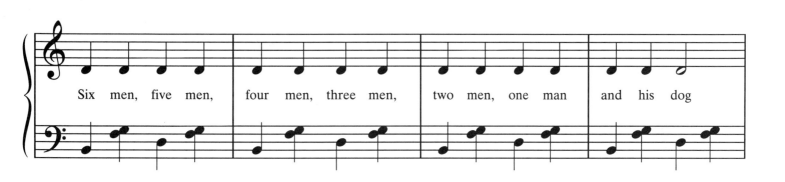

One Man Went to Mow - 4 - 4
0578B

ORANGES AND LEMONS

TRADITIONAL
Arranged by DAN COATES

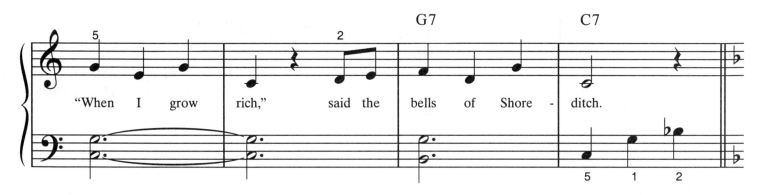

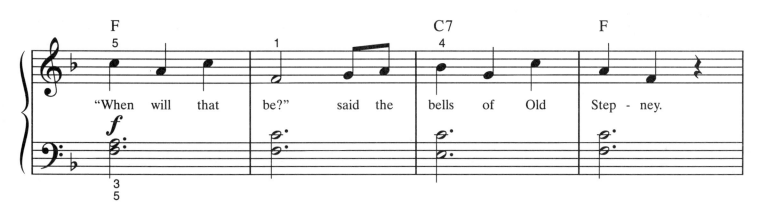

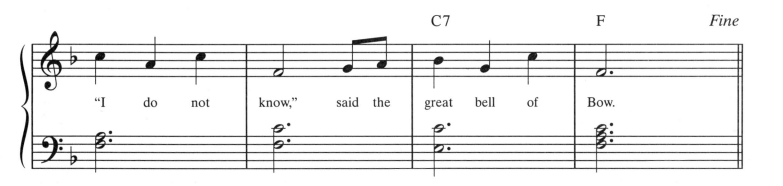

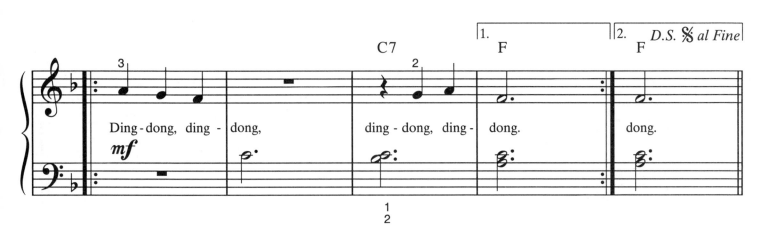

PAT-A-CAKE PAT-A-CAKE

TRADITIONAL
Arranged by DAN COATES

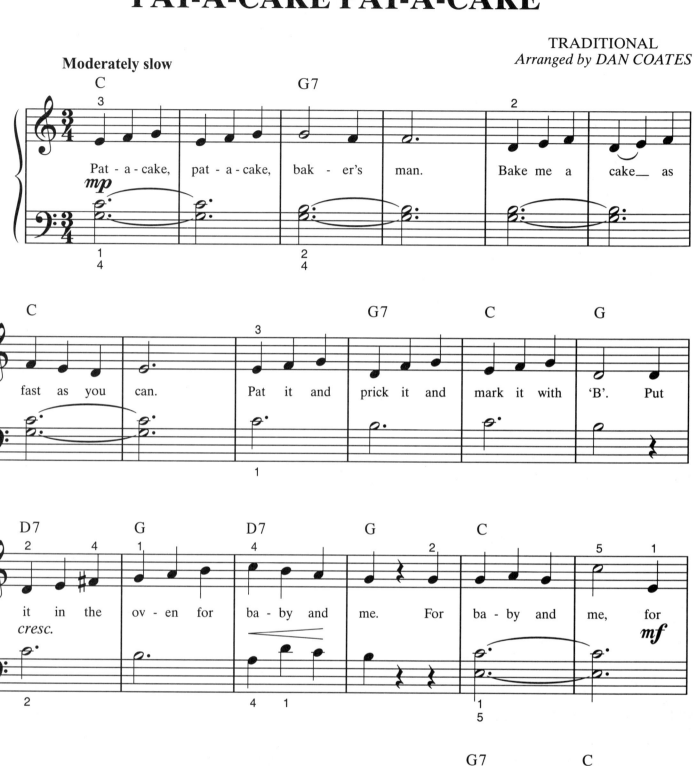

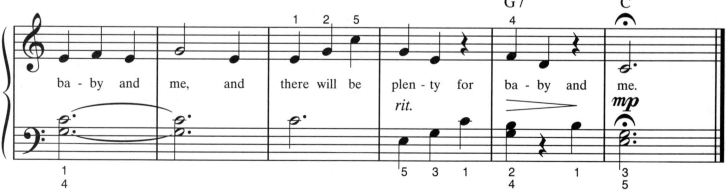

0578B

PEAS PUDDING

TRADITIONAL
Arranged by DAN COATES

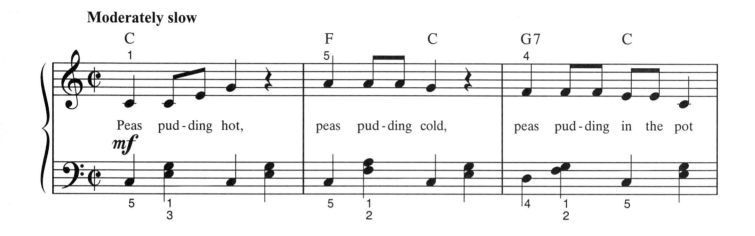

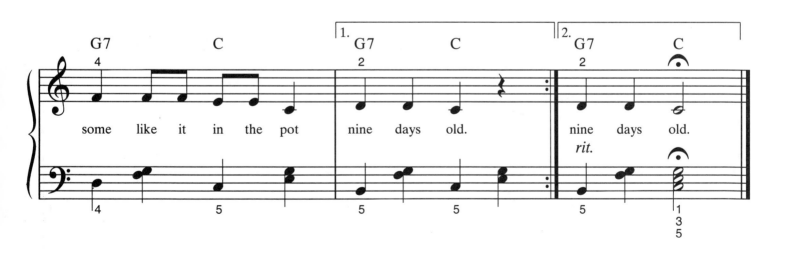

0578B

POP GOES THE WEASEL

TRADITIONAL
Arranged by DAN COATES

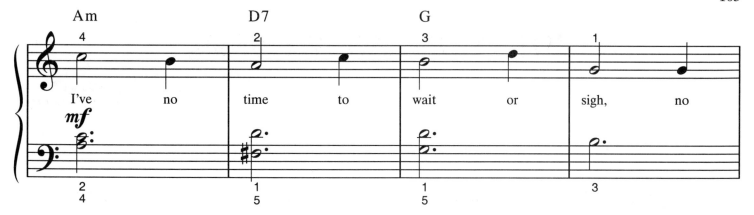

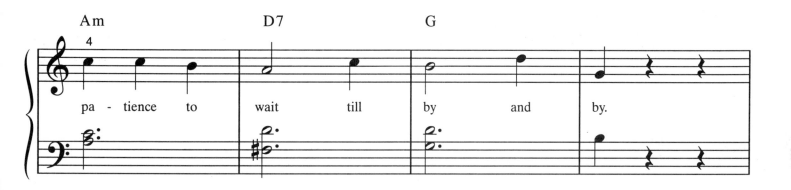

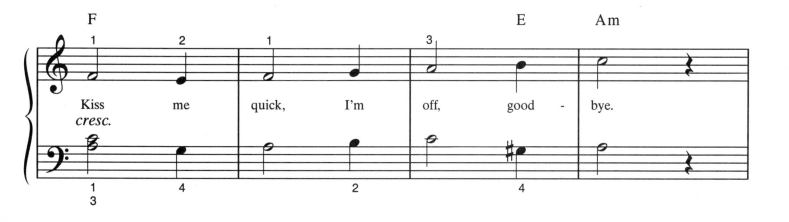

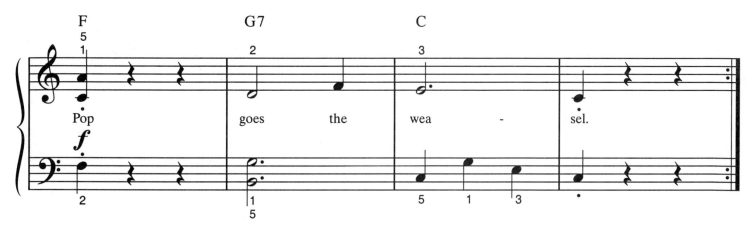

POLLY WOLLY DOODLE

TRADITIONAL
Arranged by DAN COATES

Moderately, in two

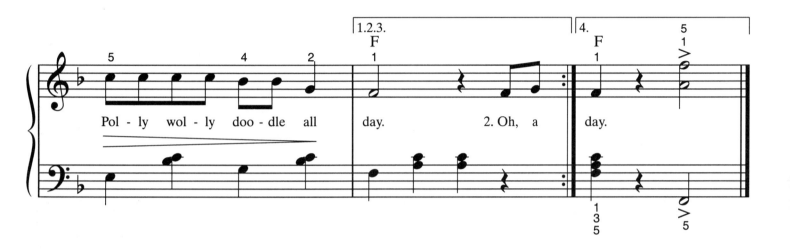

Verse 2:
Oh, a grasshopper sittin' on a railroad track,
Singing Polly wolly doodle all day,
A-pickin' his teeth with a carpet tack,
Singing Polly wolly doodle all day.
(To Chorus:)

Verse 3:
Oh, I went down South to see my Sal,
Singing Polly wolly doodle all day,
My Sal, she is a spunky gal,
Singing Polly wolly doodle all day.
(To Chorus:)

Verse 4:
Behind the barn, down on my knees,
Singing Polly wolly doodle all day.
I thought I heard a chicken sneeze,
Singing Polly wolly doodle all day.
(To Chorus:)

RIDE A COCK-HORSE TO BANBURY CROSS

TRADITIONAL
Arranged by DAN COATES

RING-A-RING-A-ROSES

TRADITIONAL
Arranged by DAN COATES

0578B

ROCK-A-BYE BABY

TRADITIONAL
Arranged by DAN COATES

0578B

ROW, ROW, ROW YOUR BOAT

TRADITIONAL
Arranged by DAN COATES

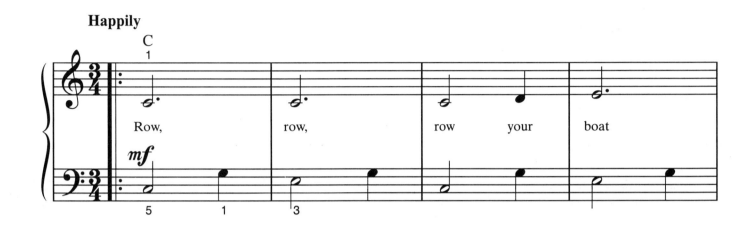

Row, row, row your boat

gent - ly   down   the   stream.

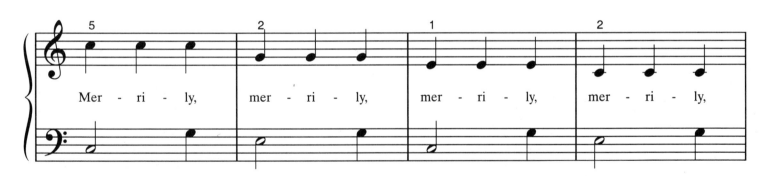

Mer - ri - ly,   mer - ri - ly,   mer - ri - ly,   mer - ri - ly,

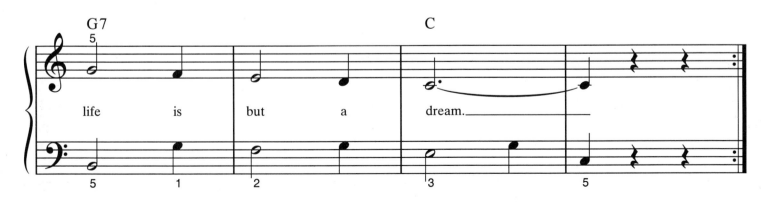

life   is   but   a   dream._____

0578B

RUB-A-DUB DUB, THREE MEN IN A TUB

TRADITIONAL
Arranged by DAN COATES

0578B

SEE-SAW MARGERY DAW

TRADITIONAL
Arranged by DAN COATES

0578B

SHE'LL BE COMING 'ROUND THE MOUNTAIN

TRADITIONAL
Arranged by DAN COATES

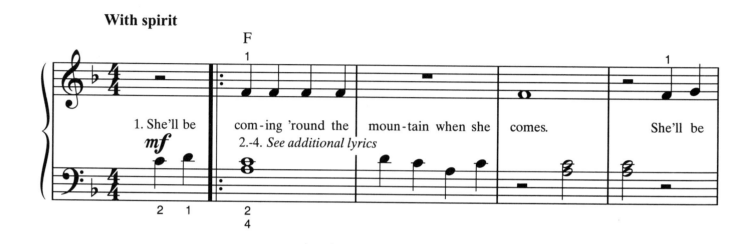

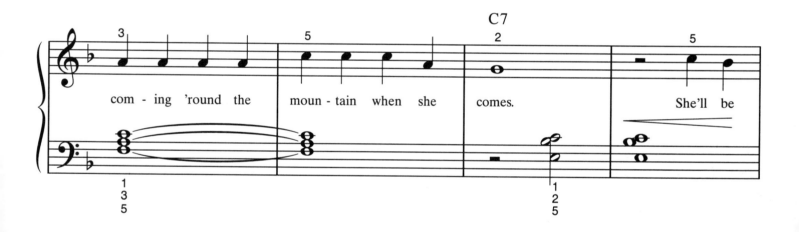

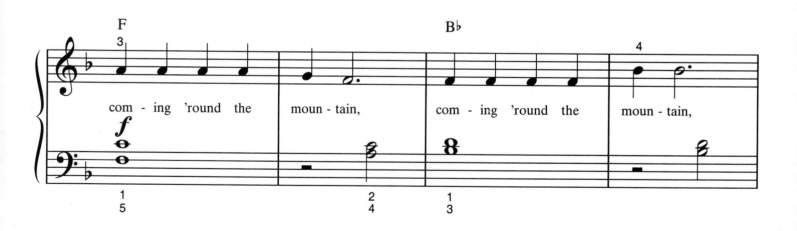

She'll Be Coming 'Round the Mountain - 2 - 1
0578B

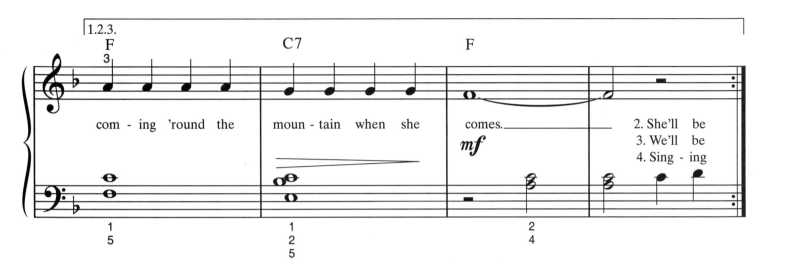

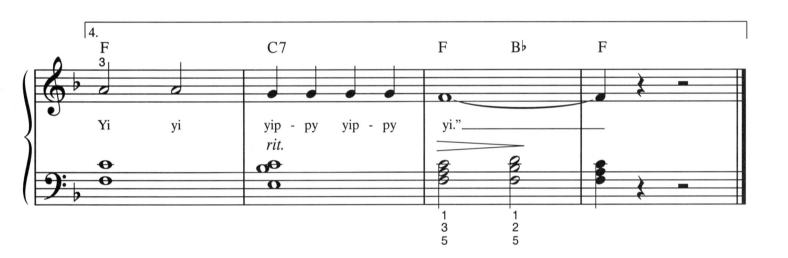

Verse 2:
She'll be driving six white horses when she comes. (Yeehah!)
She'll be driving six white horses when she comes. (Yeehah!)
She'll be driving six white horses, driving six white horses,
Driving six white horses when she comes.

Verse 3:
We'll be shouting "Hallelujah" when she comes. (Hallelujah!)
We'll be shouting "Hallelujah" when she comes. (Hallelujah!)
We'll be shouting "Hallelujah," shouting "Hallelujah,"
Shouting "Hallelujah" when she comes.

Verse 4:
Singing "Yi yi yippy yippy yi." *(Yippy yi!)*
Singing "Yi yi yippy yippy yi." *(Yippy yi!)*
Singing "Yi yi yippy, yi yi yippy,
Yi yi yippy yippy yi."

SIMPLE SIMON

TRADITIONAL
Arranged by DAN COATES

Brightly ("in two")

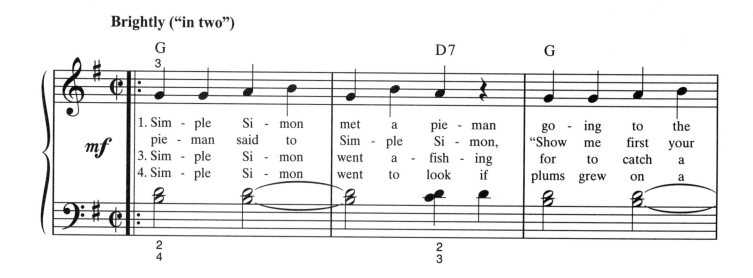

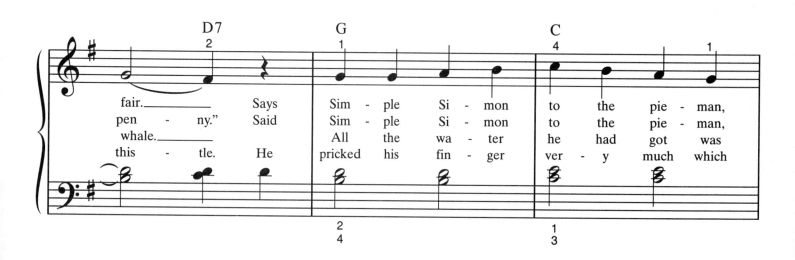

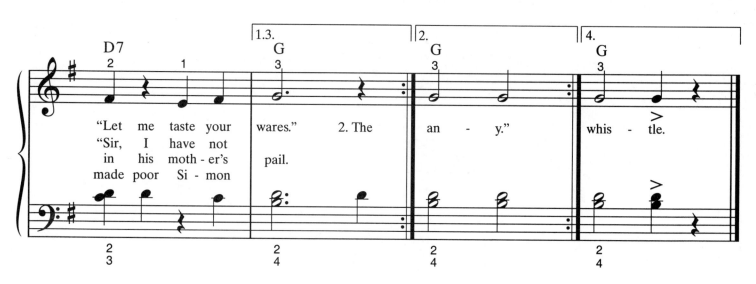

SING A SONG OF SIXPENCE

TRADITIONAL
Arranged by DAN COATES

Verse 2:
The king was in his counting house,
Counting out his money.
The queen was in the parlor,
Eating bread and honey.
The maid was in the garden,
Hanging out the clothes,
And down came a blackbird
And pecked off her nose.

0578B

SIX IN A BED

TRADITIONAL
Arranged by DAN COATES

THERE WAS A CROOKED MAN

TRADITIONAL
Arranged by DAN COATES

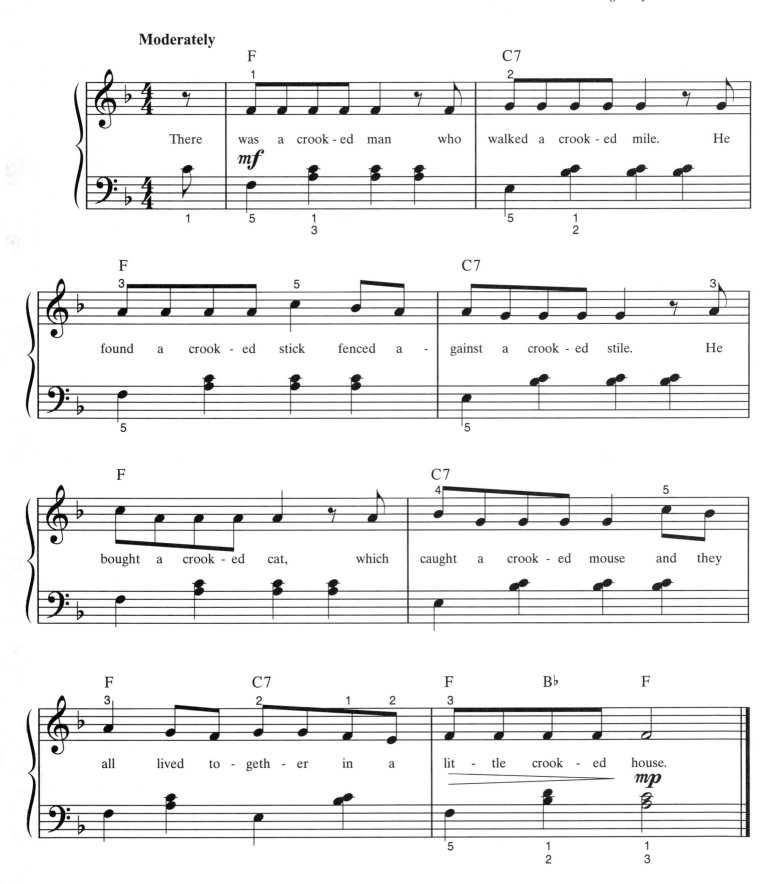

0578B

SKIP TO MY LOU

TRADITIONAL
Arranged by DAN COATES

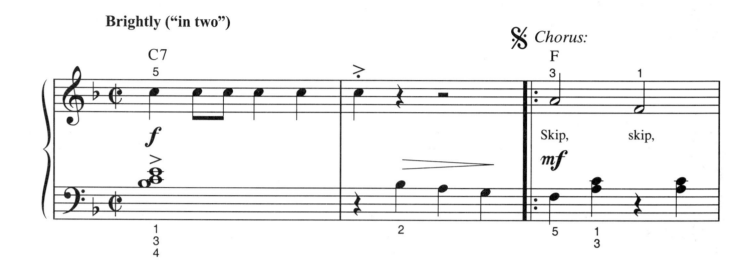

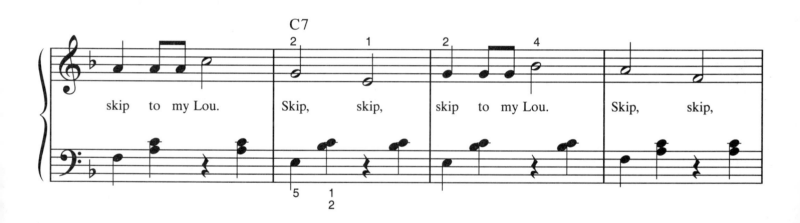

Verse:

1. Lost my part - ner. What will I do? Lost my part - ner.
2.3.4. *See additional lyrics*

What will I do? Lost my part - ner. What will I do?

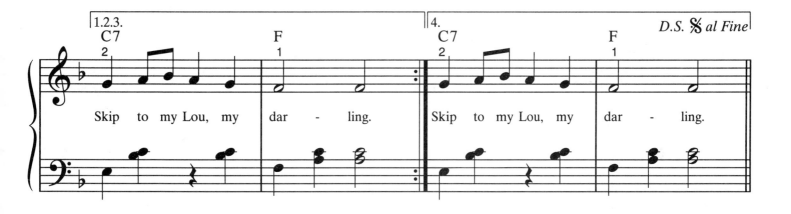

Skip to my Lou, my dar - ling. Skip to my Lou, my dar - ling.

Verse 2:
Found another one, prettier, too.
Found another one, prettier, too.
Found another one, prettier, too.
Skip to my Lou, my darling.
(To Chorus:)

Verse 3:
Can't get a redbird, bluebird'll do.
Can't get a redbird, bluebird'll do.
Can't get a redbird, bluebird'll do.
Skip to my Lou, my darling.
(To Chorus:)

Verse 4:
Flies in the sugar bowl, shoo, shoo, shoo!
Flies in the sugar bowl, shoo, shoo, shoo!
Flies in the sugar bowl, shoo, shoo, shoo!
Skip to my Lou, my darling.
(To Chorus:)

SKYE BOAT SONG

TRADITIONAL
Arranged by DAN COATES

Moderately bright waltz

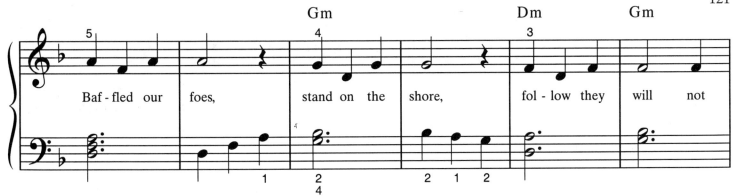

Baf - fled our foes, stand on the shore, fol - low they will not

Chorus:

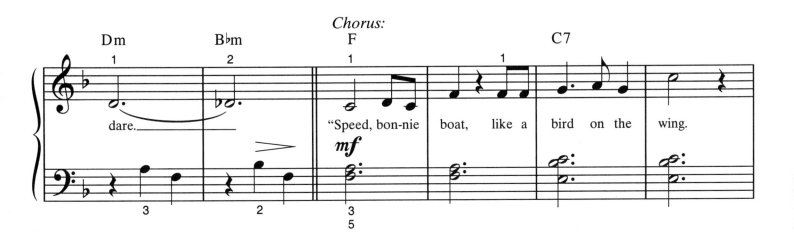

dare.____ "Speed, bon-nie boat, like a bird on the wing.

mf

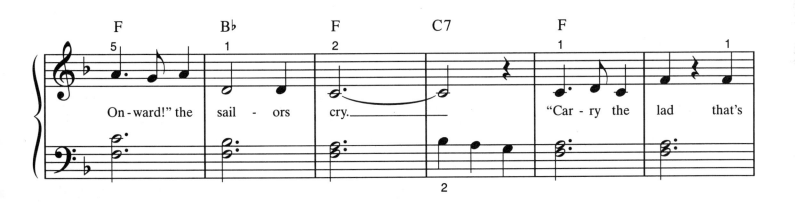

On - ward!" the sail - ors cry.____ "Car - ry the lad that's

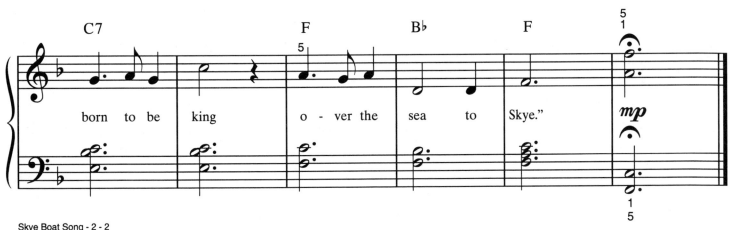

born to be king o - ver the sea to Skye."

mp

'TWAS ON A MONDAY MORNING

TRADITIONAL
Arranged by DAN COATES

Brightly, with spirit

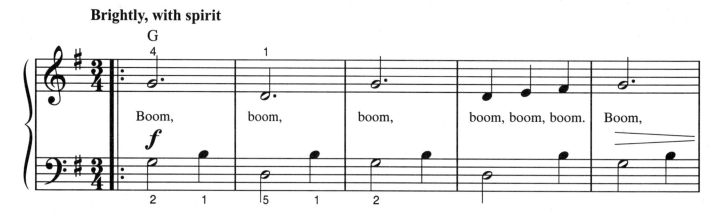

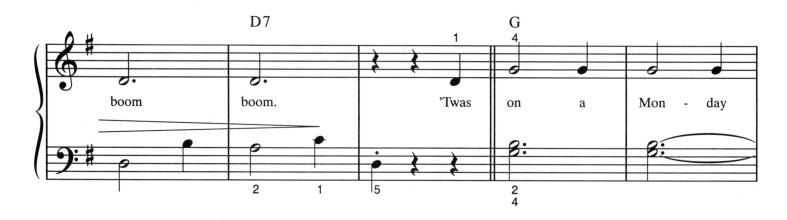

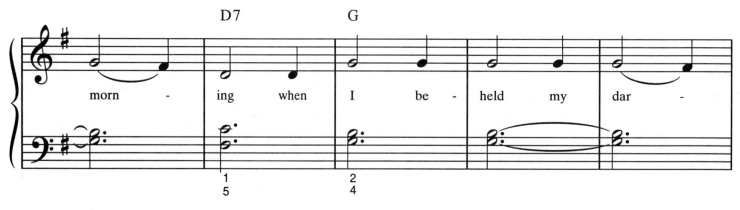

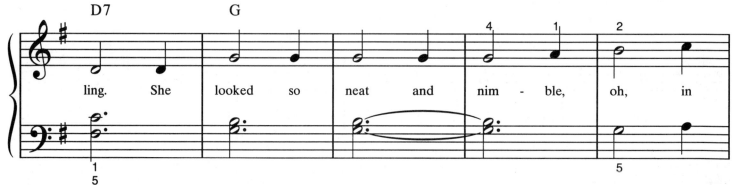

'Twas on a Monday Morning - 2 - 1
0578B

TAKE ME OUT TO THE BALL GAME

Words by JACK NORWORTH
Music by ALBERT VON TIZLER
Arranged by DAN COATES

Bright waltz

THERE'S A HOLE IN MY BUCKET

TRADITIONAL
Arranged by DAN COATES

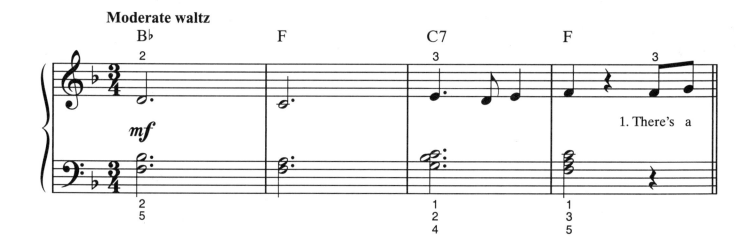

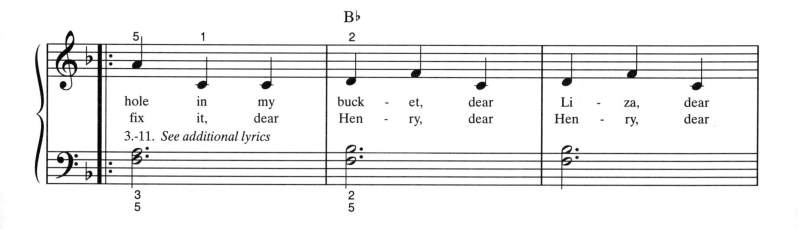

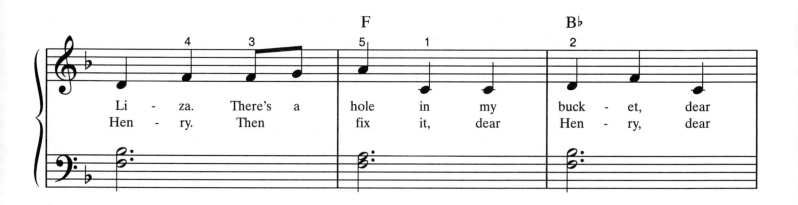

There's a Hole in My Bucket - 2 - 1
0578B

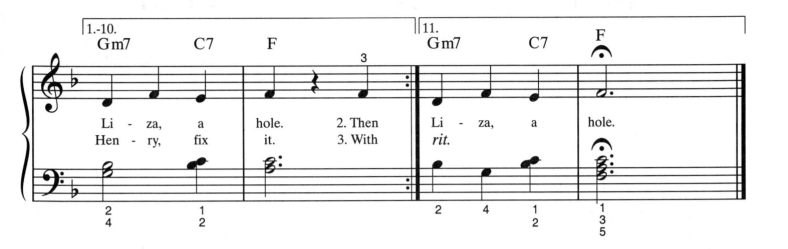

Verse 3:
With what shall I fix it,
Dear Liza, dear Liza?
With what shall I fix it,
Dear Liza, with what?

Verse 4:
With straw, dear Henry,
Dear Henry, dear Henry.
With straw, dear Henry,
Dear Henry, with straw.

Verse 5:
But the straw is too long,
Dear Liza, dear Liza.
But the straw is too long,
Dear Liza, too long.

Verse 6:
Then cut it dear Henry,
Dear Henry, dear Henry.
Then cut it, dear Henry,
Dear Henry, cut it.

Verse 7:
But the knife is too blunt,
Dear Liza, dear Liza.
But the knife is too blunt,
Dear Liza, too blunt.

Verse 8:
Then sharpen it, dear Henry,
Dear Henry, dear Henry.
Then sharpen it, dear Henry,
Dear Henry, sharpen it.

Verse 9:
But the stone is too dry,
Dear Liza, dear Liza.
But the stone is too dry,
Dear Liza, too dry.

Verse 10:
Then wet it, dear Henry,
Dear Henry, dear Henry.
Then wet it, dear Henry,
Dear Henry, wet it.

Verse 11:
There's a hole in my bucket,
Dear Liza, dear Liza.
There's a hole in my bucket,
Dear Liza, a hole.

THIS IS THE WAY THE LADIES RIDE

TRADITIONAL
Arranged by DAN COATES

Verses 3 & 4:

THIS OLD MAN (KNICK-KNACK PADDY WACK)

TRADITIONAL
Arranged by DAN COATES

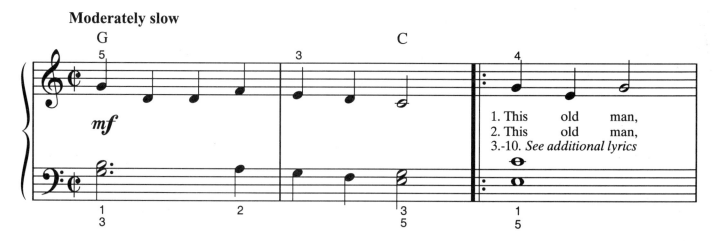

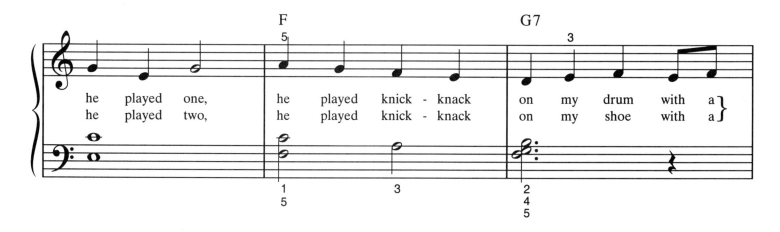

This Old Man (Knick-Knack Paddy Wack) - 2 - 1
0578B

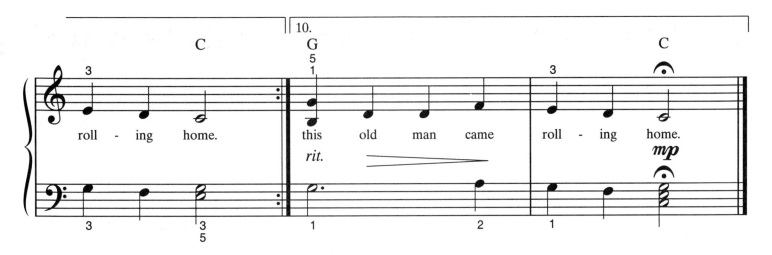

Verse 3:
This old man, he played three,
He played knick-knack on my knee
With a knick-knack paddy wack
Give a dog a bone,
This old man came rolling home.

Verse 4:
This old man, he played four,
He played knick-knack on my door
With a knick-knack paddy wack
Give a dog a bone,
This old man came rolling home.

Verse 5:
This old man, he played five,
He played knick-knack on my hive
With a knick-knack paddy wack
Give a dog a bone,
This old man came rolling home.

Verse 6:
This old man, he played six,
He played knick-knack on my sticks
With a knick-knack paddy wack
Give a dog a bone,
This old man came rolling home.

Verse 7:
This old man, he played seven,
He played knick-knack up to heaven
With a knick-knack paddy wack
Give a dog a bone,
This old man came rolling home.

Verse 8:
This old man, he played eight,
He played knick-knack on my gate
With a knick-knack paddy wack
Give a dog a bone,
This old man came rolling home.

Verse 9:
This old man, he played nine,
He played knick-knack on my line
With a knick-knack paddy wack
Give a dog a bone,
This old man came rolling home.

Verse 10:
This old man, he played ten,
He played knick-knack over again
With a knick-knack paddy wack
Give a dog a bone,
This old man came rolling home.

This Old Man (Knick-Knack Paddy Wack) - 2 - 2
0578B

THREE BLIND MICE

TRADITIONAL
Arranged by DAN COATES

Three Blind Mice - 2 - 1
0578B

THREE LITTLE PIGS

TRADITIONAL
Arranged by DAN COATES

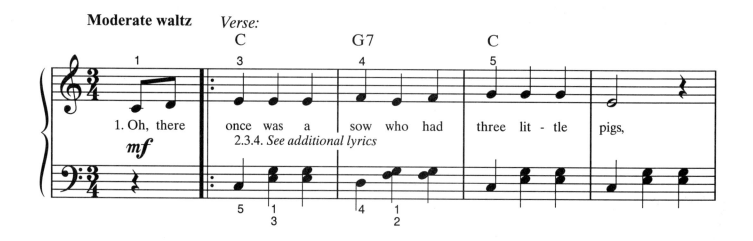

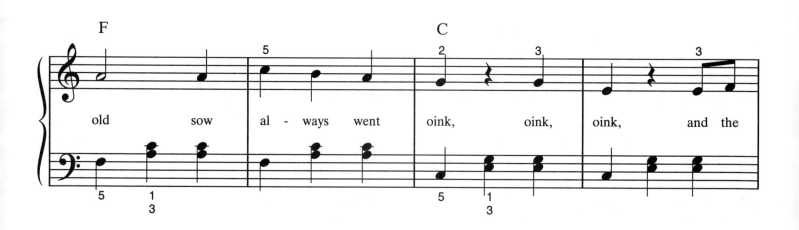

Three Little Pigs - 2 - 1
0578B

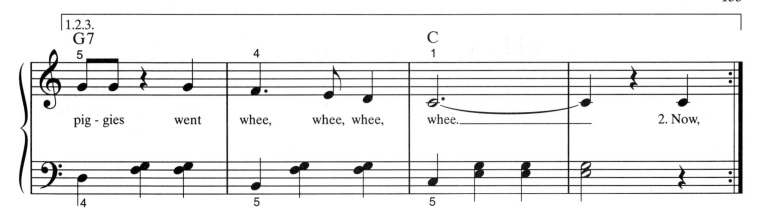

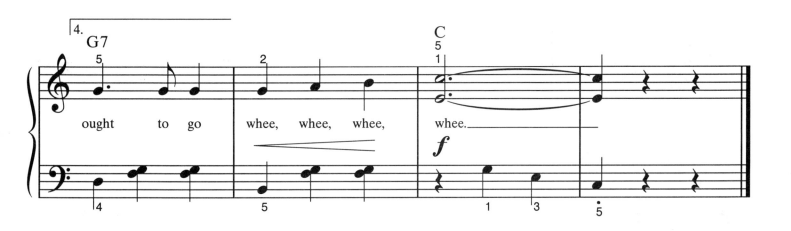

Verse 2:
Now, one day one of the three little pigs
To the other two piggies, said he,
"Why don't we always go oink, oink, oink?
It's so childish to go whee, whee, whee, whee."

Verse 3:
These three piggies grew skinny and lean.
Skinny they well should be
For they always would try to go oink, oink, oink,
And they wouldn't go whee, whee, whee, whee.

Verse 4:
Now, these three piggies, they upped and they died,
A very sad sight to see.
So don't ever try to go oink, oink, oink,
When you ought to go whee, whee, whee, whee.

THREE LITTLE KITTENS

TRADITIONAL
Arranged by DAN COATES

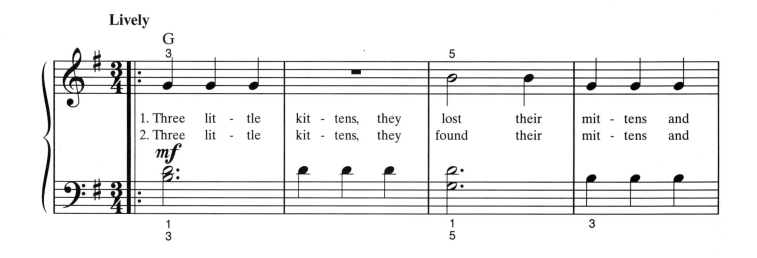

1. Three lit - tle kit - tens, they lost their mit - tens and
2. Three lit - tle kit - tens, they found their mit - tens and

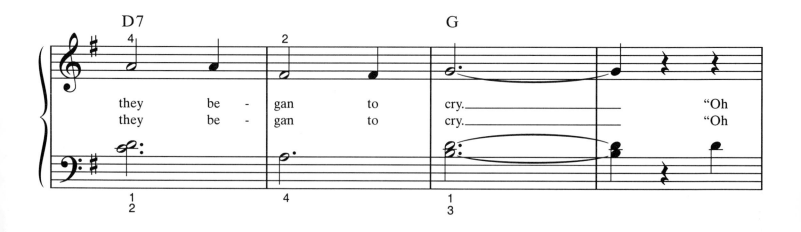

they be - gan to cry.___ "Oh
they be - gan to cry.___ "Oh

Moth - er, dear, we sad - ly fear that
Moth - er, dear, we see here, see here, for

Three Little Kittens - 3 - 1
0578B

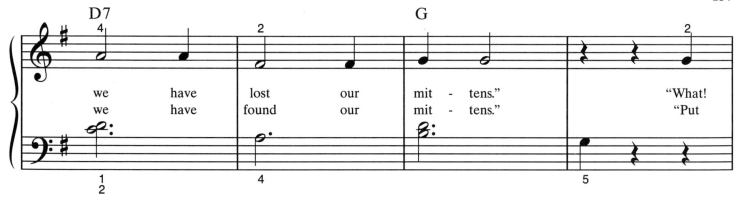

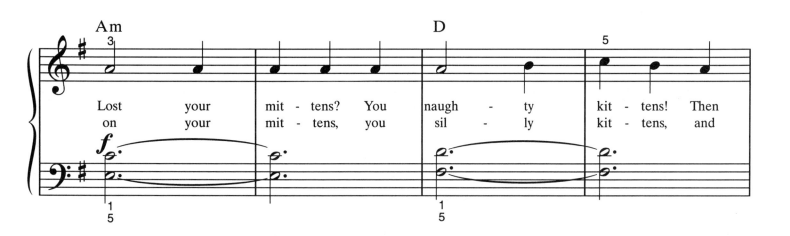

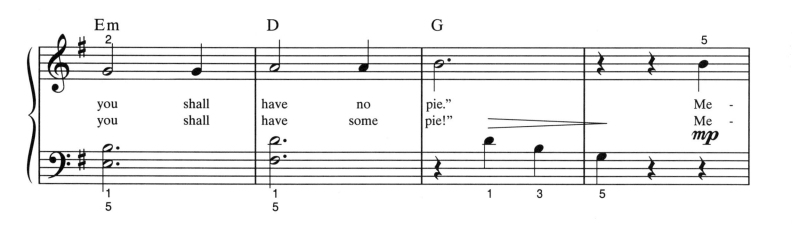

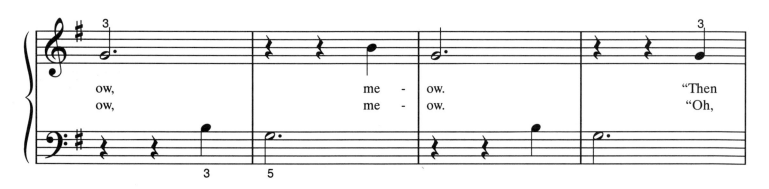

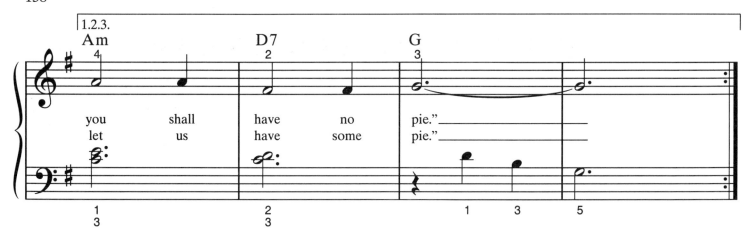

1.2.3.

you shall have no pie."
let us have some pie."

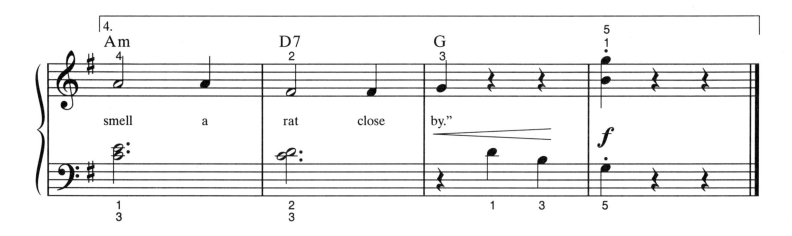

4.

smell a rat close by."

Verse 3:
Three little kittens put on their mittens
And soon ate up the pie.
"Oh Mother, dear, we greatly fear
That we have soiled our mittens."
"What? Soiled your mittens?
You naughty kittens!"
Then they began to sigh.
Meow, meow.
Then they began to sigh.

Verse 4:
Three little kittens, they washed their mittens
And hung them out to dry.
"Oh Mother, dear, do you not hear
That we have washed our mittens?"
"What? Washed your mittens?
Then you're good kittens!
But I smell a rat close by."
Meow, meow.
"We smell a rat close by."

TOM, TOM THE PIPER'S SON

TRADITIONAL
Arranged by DAN COATES

Moderately slow

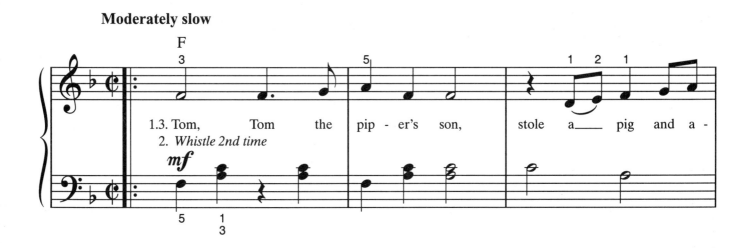

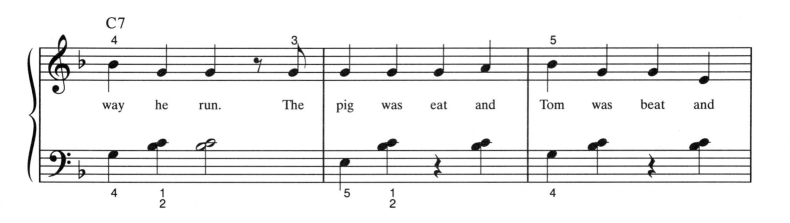

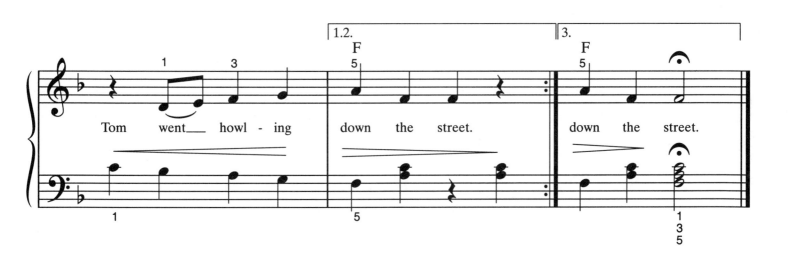

0578B

TO MARKET TO MARKET

TRADITIONAL
Arranged by DAN COATES

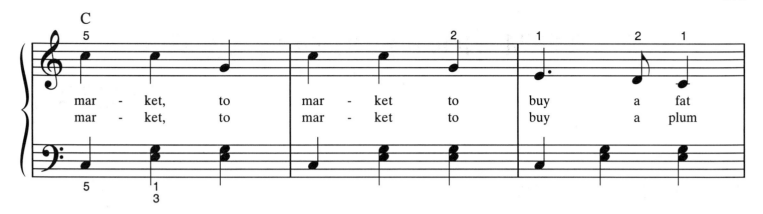

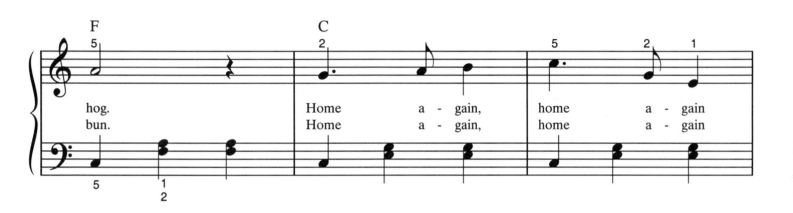

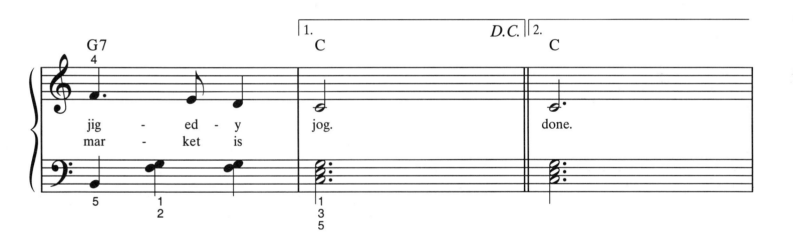

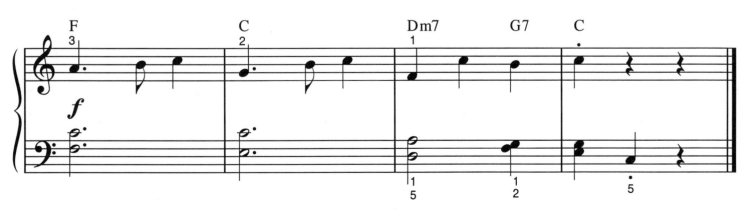

TWINKLE, TWINKLE LITTLE STAR

TRADITIONAL
Arranged by DAN COATES

Moderately slow, with expression

0578B

YANKEE DOODLE

TRADITIONAL
Arranged by DAN COATES

0578B

WALTZING MATILDA

TRADITIONAL
Arranged by DAN COATES

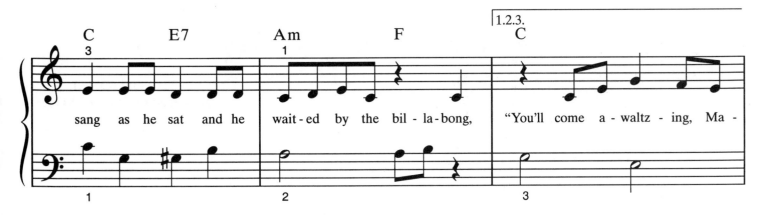

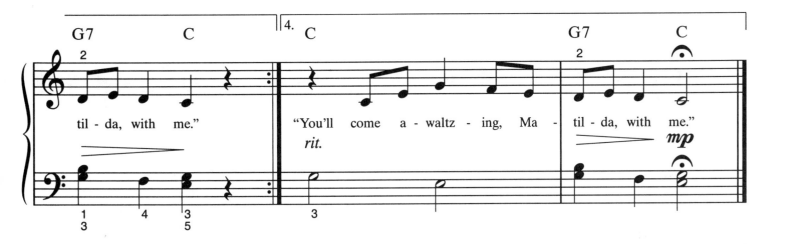

Verse 2:
Down came a jumbuck to drink beside the billabong,
Up jumped the swagman and seized him with glee,
And he sang as he talked to that jumbuck in his tucker bag,
"You'll come a-waltzing, Matilda, with me."

Chorus 2:
"Waltzing Matilda, waltzing Matilda,
You'll come a-waltzing, Matilda, with me."
And he sang as he talked to that jumbuck in his tucker bag,
"You'll come a-waltzing, Matilda, with me."

Verse 3:
Down came the stalk man, riding on his thoroughbred,
Down came the troopers, One, two, three.
"Where's that jolly jumbuck you've got in your tucker bag?
You'll come a-waltzing, Matilda, with me."

Chorus 3:
"Waltzing Matilda, waltzing Matilda,
You'll come a-waltzing, Matilda, with me."
"Where's that jolly jumbuck you've got in your tucker bag?
You'll come a-waltzing, Matilda, with me."

Verse 4:
Up jumped the swagman, and plunged into the billabong.
"You'll never catch me alive," cried he.
And his ghost may be heard as you ride beside the billabong,
"You'll come a-waltzing, Matilda, with me."

Chorus 4:
"Waltzing Matilda, waltzing Matilda,
You'll come a-waltzing, Matilda, with me."
And his ghost may be heard as you ride beside the billabong,
"You'll come a-waltzing, Matilda, with me."

WINKUM, WINKUM

TRADITIONAL
Arranged by DAN COATES

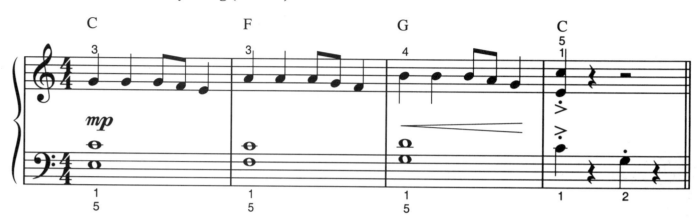

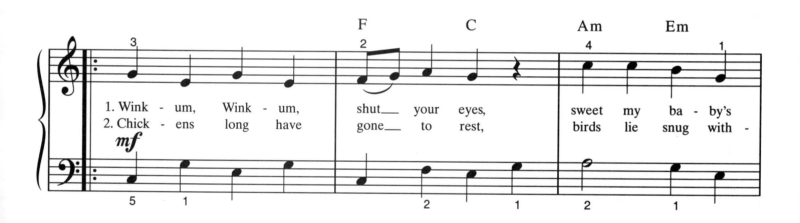

1. Wink - um, Wink - um, shut___ your eyes, sweet my ba - by's
2. Chick - ens long have gone___ to rest, birds lie snug with -

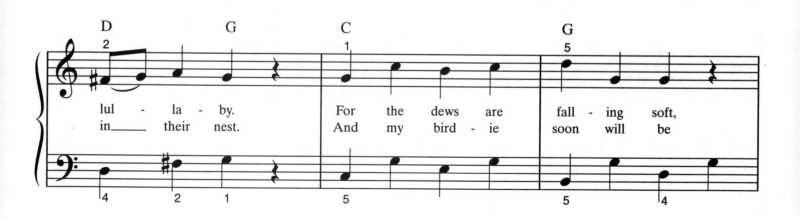

lul - la - by. For the dews are fall - ing soft,
in___ their nest. And my bird - ie soon will be

Winkum, Winkum - 2 - 1
0578B

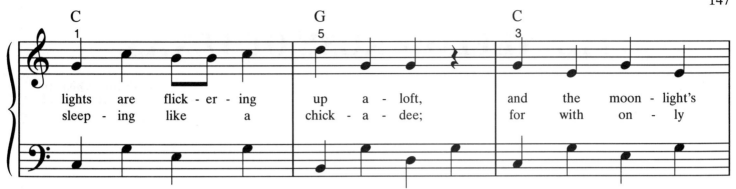

lights are flick - er - ing up a - loft, and the moon - light's
sleep - ing like a chick - a - dee; for with on - ly

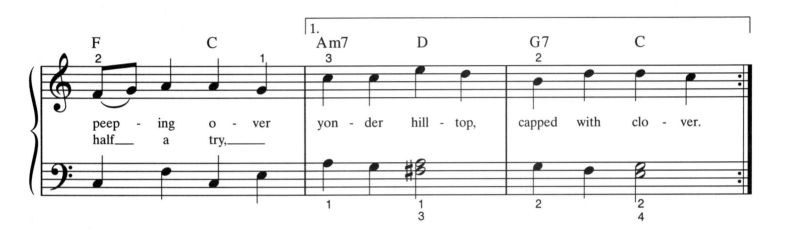

peep - ing o - ver yon - der hill - top, capped with clo - ver.
half___ a try,_____

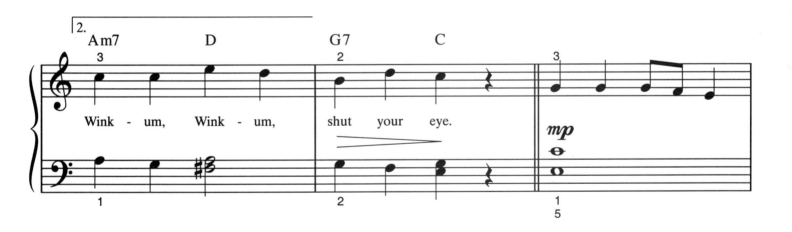

Wink - um, Wink - um, shut your eye.

THE YELLOW ROSE OF TEXAS

Words and Music by
DON GEORGE
Arranged by DAN COATES

Bright, steady tempo

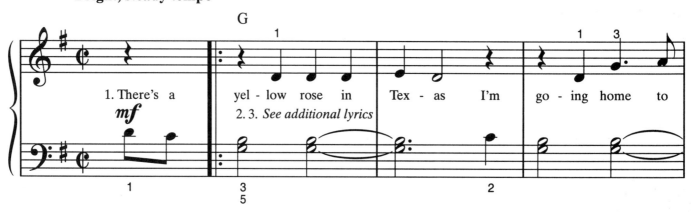

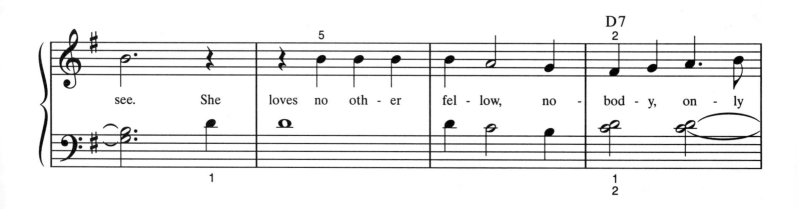

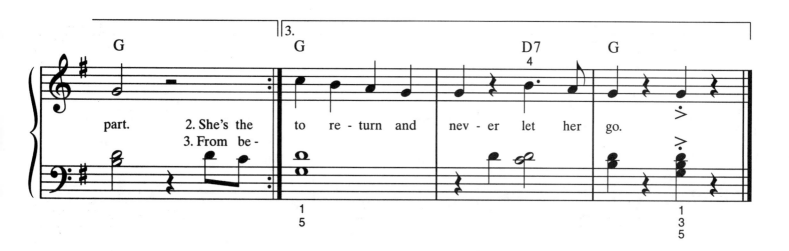

Verse 2:
She's the sweetest little lady
A fellow ever knew.
Her eyes are bright as diamonds,
They sparkle like the dew.
You may talk about your dearest girls
And sing of Rosalie,
But the Yellow Rose of Texas
Beats the belles of Tennessee.

Verse 3:
From beside the Rio Grande
The stars were shining bright.
We walked along together
One quiet summer night.
I hope she will remember
How we parted long ago.
I'll keep my promise to return
And never let her go.

YOU ARE MY SUNSHINE

Words and Music by
JIMMIE DAVIS
and CHARLES MITCHELL
Arranged by DAN COATES

BINGO

TRADITIONAL
Arranged by DAN COATES

Verse 3:
There was a farmer had a dog
And Bingo was his name-o.
(Clap, clap) n-g-o.
(Clap, clap) n-g-o.
(Clap, clap) n-g-o.
And Bingo was his name-o.

Verse 4:
There was a farmer had a dog
And Bingo was his name-o.
(Clap, clap, clap) g-o.
(Clap, clap, clap) g-o.
(Clap, clap, clap) g-o.
And Bingo was his name-o.

Verse 5:
There was a farmer had a dog
And Bingo was his name-o.
(Clap, clap, clap, clap) o.
(Clap, clap, clap, clap) o.
(Clap, clap, clap, clap) o.
And Bingo was his name-o.

Verse 6:
There was a farmer had a dog
And Bingo was his name-o.
(Clap, clap, clap, clap, clap).
(Clap, clap, clap, clap, clap).
(Clap, clap, clap, clap, clap).
And Bingo was his name-o.

0578B

FRERE JACQUES

TRADITIONAL
Arranged by DAN COATES

Moderately slow

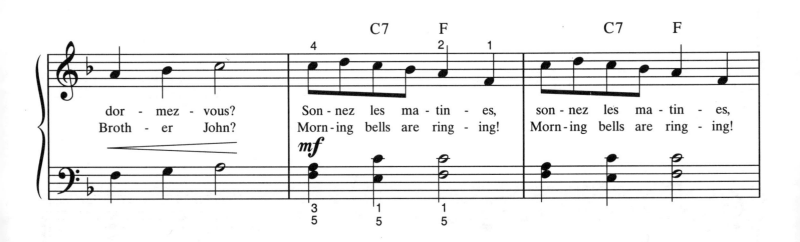

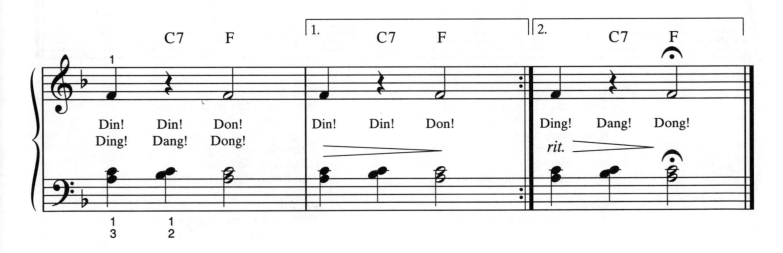

GOD BLESS THE MOON

TRADITIONAL
Arranged by DAN COATES

0578B

THIS LITTLE PIG

TRADITIONAL
Arranged by DAN COATES

POLLY, PUT THE KETTLE ON

TRADITIONAL
Arranged by DAN COATES

0578B

Dan Coates

As a student at the University of Miami, Dan Coates paid his tuition by playing the piano at south Florida nightclubs and restaurants. One evening in 1975, after Dan had worked his unique brand of magic on the ivories, a stranger from the music field walked up and told him that he should put his inspired piano arrangements down on paper so they could be published.

Dan took the stranger's advice—and the world of music has become much richer as a result. Since that chance encounter long ago, Dan has gone on to achieve international acclaim for his brilliant piano arrangements. His *Big Note, Easy Piano* and *Professional Touch* arrangements have inspired countless piano students and established themselves as classics against which all other works must be measured.

Enjoying an exclusive association with Warner Bros. Publications since 1982, Dan has demonstrated a unique gift for writing arrangements intended for students of every level, from beginner to advanced. Dan never fails to bring a fresh and original approach to his work. Pushing his own creative boundaries with each new manuscript, he writes material that is musically exciting and educationally sound.

From the very beginning of his musical life, Dan has always been eager to seek new challenges. As a five-year-old in Syracuse, New York, he used to sneak into the home of his neighbors to play their piano. Blessed with an amazing ear for music, Dan was able to imitate the melodies of songs he had heard on the radio. Finally, his neighbors convinced his parents to buy Dan his own piano. At that point, there was no stopping his musical development. Dan won a prestigious New York State competition for music composers at the age of 15. Then, after graduating from high school, he toured the world as an arranger and pianist with the group Up With People.

Later, Dan studied piano at the University of Miami with the legendary Ivan Davis, developing his natural abilities to stylize music on the keyboard. Continuing to perform professionally during and after his college years, Dan has played the piano on national television and at the 1984 Summer Olympics in Los Angeles. He has also accompanied recording artists as diverse as Dusty Springfield and Charlotte Rae.

During his long and prolific association with Warner Bros. Publications, Dan has written many award-winning books. He conducts piano workshops worldwide, demonstrating his famous arrangements with a special spark that never fails to inspire students and teachers alike.